THE CRITICS D

General Editor Michael Scott

TESS OF THE D'URBERVILLES

Terence Wright

M
MACMILLAN
EDUCATION

First published in 1987
Reprinted 1988

Published by
MACMILLAN EDUCATION LTD
Houndmills, Basingstoke, Hampshire RG21 2XS
and London
Companies and representatives
throughout the world

Printed in Hong Kong

Wright, Terence
Thomas Hardy, Tess of the d'Urbervilles.—(The Critics Debate)
1. Hardy, Thomas, Tess of the d'Urbervilles
I. Title II. Series
823'.8 PR4748
ISBN 0-333-39583-2
ISBN 0-333-39584-0 Pbk

Contents

General Editor's Preface

OVER THE last few years the practice of literary criticism has become hotly debated. Methods developed earlier in the century and before have been attacked and the word 'crisis' has been drawn upon to describe the present condition of English Studies. That such a debate is taking place is a sign of the subject discipline's health. Some would hold that the situation necessitates a radical alternative approach which naturally implies a 'crisis situation'. Others would respond that to employ such terms is to precipitate or construct a false position. The debate continues but it is not the first. 'New Criticism' acquired its title because it attempted something fresh calling into question certain practices of the past. Yet the practices it attacked were not entirely lost or negated by the new critics. One factor becomes clear: English Studies is a pluralistic discipline.

What are students coming to advanced work in English for the first time to make of all this debate and controversy? They are in danger of being overwhelmed by the cross currents of critical approaches as they take up their study of literature. The purpose of this series is to help delineate various critical approaches to specific literary texts. Its authors are from a variety of critical schools and have approached their task in a flexible manner. Their aim is to help the reader come to terms with the variety of criticism and to introduce him or her to further reading on the subject and to a fuller evaluation of a particular text by illustrating the way it has been approached in a number of contexts. In the first part of the book a critical survey is given of some of the major ways the text has been appraised. This is done sometimes in a thematic manner, sometimes according to various 'schools' or 'approaches'. In the second part the authors provide their own appraisals of the text from their stated critical standpoint, allowing the reader the knowledge of their own particular approaches from which their views may in turn be evaluated. The series therein hopes to introduce and to elucidate criticism of authors and texts being studied and to encourage participation as the critics debate.

vii

Michael Scott

A Note on Text and References

ALL references to *Tess of the d'Urbervilles* are to the Penguin edition, edited by David Skilton (Harmondsworth, 1978), and are given in square brackets. References to secondary material appear in parentheses with date of publication on the introduction of each such work. Details may then be found in the 'References' section, where secondary works are listed in the order of first citation in the text.

Introduction

AFTER nearly one hundred years of diverse, complex and celebratory criticism it may seem surprising that the first 'critical debate' on *Tess of the d'Urbervilles* concerned itself with something (to us) of such peripheral interest as the book's narrowly moral effect upon susceptible readers. At almost the last moment Hardy added a subtitle – 'A Pure Woman' – and the choice of adjective would seem to have been made in order to defy the moral prejudices of the more squeamish readers of 1891 and fire another shot in a battle which had begun some time before.

In common with most successful novelists of his age, it was Hardy's practice to write first for one of the popular magazines, which, with their wide circulations, were the most lucrative medium for publishing fiction at the time. Only when the novel was well launched in serial form would it appear as a single volume. In the case of *Tess* Hardy had agreed publication with Tillotson and Son of Bolton, who had accepted this contract from England's leading novelist without asking to see any outline of the story. It was only when they had received a considerable portion of the work that they found the subject matter unsuitable, not only for their firm to print (they were traditionally strong Nonconformists) but also for 'family reading' (that is, for women and children). Hardy would not modify the tale, and it was therefore amicably agreed to terminate the contract.

If Hardy thought he could simply publish elsewhere he was soon to find otherwise. He had to suffer the humiliation of two more refusals, by *Murray's* and *Macmillan's* magazines, before *Tess* was accepted by the *Graphic* for 1891. Moreover, to gain acceptance the author was forced to mutilate his story so that supposedly offensive passages would not remain to disturb the 'family reader'. Tess was therefore made the dupe of a mock marriage, and the baptism of her baby was entirely excised. In a notoriously ridiculous change Angel resorted to a wheelbarrow to ferry the milkmaids along the flooded road, rather than carrying them in his arms. Only publication of the book as a separate whole allowed the author to reinstate the text he had originally submitted, and, while many reviews were favourable, there were still those who could say he had told 'an unpleasant story in a very unpleasant way'.

By 1912 Hardy could say he regretted the subtitle, but in 1892 he felt the moral implications of the word 'pure' strongly and personally enough to enter the fray on his own behalf, declaring in the Preface to the fifth edition that many critics revealed an inability to associate the idea of the word 'with any but the artificial and derivative meaning which has resulted to it from the ordinances of civilization. They ignore the meaning of the word in Nature . . .' The suggested conflict between civilisation and Nature is one which, as we shall see, was to be taken by a number of critics as a central theme of the novel.

But Hardy's personal commitment to his novel went beyond mere questions of textual integrity. In addition to the subtitle he appended at proof stage an epigraph from Shakespeare:

> . . . Poor wounded name! My bosom as a bed
> Shall lodge thee.

Taken with the designation 'pure', this suggests a defensiveness about the heroine herself on the author's part, and indeed it seems that Hardy was concerned with her good name almost as though she were a real person. Reasons may be found for this personal involvement in the genesis of Tess as a character. The name which Hardy eventually decided on for his heroine was taken from that of his cousin, Teresa Hardy, who said that 'the main episodes happened to a relative of theirs'. Robert Gittings (1978) believes it is 'practically certain' that this relative was 'Hardy's much loved grandmother'. More than twenty years after her first appearance the power of this imagined girl to move her creator was demonstrated in a quite different way. In 1924 a young actress, Gertrude Bugler, played Tess in a dramatised version of the novel given by the 'Hardy Players'. Hardy was impressed by the quality of her acting, but even more by the way in which she seemed physically to resemble the idea of Tess he had long carried in his mind. Added to this was the fact that Gertrude's mother, Augusta Way, was, he said, the woman who had first suggested the figure of Tess to him when he saw her working as a milkmaid. Most interesting of all, however, it seems that Hardy, in a curious confounding of fiction and reality, fell in love with Gertrude Bugler/Tess

Durbeyfield, despite his eighty years. Seldom can a writer have so involved himself with one of his characters, but the involvement was crucial, for, if we are to feel an essential beauty in this work, it is to a large extent a beauty that comes from Tess, physically beautiful in herself and encapsulating the moral beauties of pathos, suffering and fortitude, which together lead to the ultimate, painful beauty of tragedy. Without a sense of her reality the book is nothing.

Nevertheless, Hardy's personal involvement was not with Tess alone. In autumn 1888, while he was planning his new novel, he made a trip to Woolcombe, an estate which had once belonged to an ancient family of Dorset Hardys. The novelist, always eager to trace his ancestry to distinguished forbears, believed himself distantly allied to this once-wealthy family, and was therefore struck by the decline in their fortunes, and those of his own relations. He told in his diary of seeing a tall thin man walking behind a horse and trap when he was young, and being told by his mother that the man represented what was once the leading branch of the family. 'So we go down, down, down', he added. His observation of this decline in his own family is obviously mirrored in the fictional decline of the d'Urbervilles, who are now feckless Durbeyfields, their estate and name taken by the new aristocracy of capital. On a larger scale, the sense of decline is part of that awareness of change in the long and short term which informs the whole novel. Decline specifically would have struck a strongly contemporary note in 1891, there being a pervasive feeling, supposedly backed by scientific evidence, that all things, human and natural, were hastening into decay.

I have drawn attention to the matter of ancient families because it shows that *Tess of the d'Urbervilles* is not to be seen, and was not seen by Hardy himself, as being a novel simply about the trials of the heroine. In the three words 'history', 'decline' and 'family' we have the roots of what are, as we shall see, whole fields of criticism in the twentieth century: social, historical and philosophical – the bulk in fact of what I shall refer to as 'causative' criticism, which sees the book as primarily an expression of what brings about the tragedy. This approach is more particularly discussed in the first three sections of the 'Survey' part of the book.

There is a further approach to the novel, and this is one

which regards the *form* of the work as being the chief means of 'knowing' it. It is perhaps not surprising that this is a line taken only comparatively recently by critics of *Tess*. One of the first advocates in English of such an approach to fiction was Hardy's contemporary and fellow novelist Henry James, and his judgement of *Tess* was at best patronising. He described it as 'chock-full of faults and falsity' while admitting its 'beauty and charm', and incidentally referred to the author as 'the good little Thomas Hardy'.

At that time, perhaps, the differences between the two writers were very apparent. Hardy seemed to most people (and probably to himself) a traditional storyteller in the Dickens and George Eliot mould. But critics are now far more prepared to see Hardy the major poet as guiding the hand of the major novelist, and to see *Tess* as scene and symbol, as much as story and character. 'Formal' approaches are dealt with in the fourth section, and the 'Survey' closes with a brief discussion of a scholarly and textual approach to the novel.

And yet it is to character that we must return, in the person of the heroine at least, since it is she who centres the novel's tragedy; and, if there is one thing which all critics are agreed upon, it is the tragic power of *Tess of the d'Urbervilles*. Given this, however, a central problem remains. Are we to see this tragedy as lying in the effect the heroine's experiences have on us – the so-called cathartic emotions of pity and fear? If so, how much weight, and what kind of weight, should be given to causes – historical, personal, social, cosmological – all of which have been advanced by critics in this century? Is the novel, in short, 'causative' or 'affective'? I hope to give some answer to this central question in the 'Appraisal' part of the book but first I shall try to give an outline of some of the major critical responses to *Tess of the d'Urbervilles*.

Part One
Survey

Social approaches

ALL the following approaches to the novel fall into one category, but I shall begin with those which are most strictly 'sociological', which see the meaning of the work, and more specifically the heroine's tragedy, as residing not so much in human personality, with its loves and hates, beliefs and morality, as in the forces of society, in economics and the movements of history.

An extreme statement of this position is to be found in Arnold Kettle's declaration that the subject of *Tess* is not the fate of a 'pure woman', but 'the destruction of the English peasantry'. This opinion, which at first may seem bizarre, can be supported by a good deal of evidence from the text, once one has decided to adopt a specific viewpoint. This viewpoint sees the novel as a 'moral fable' rather than a work primarily of psychological realism, and we shall return to it in a moment.

The evidence for a 'social' approach

One of the major arguments which may be adduced in favour of a 'sociological' reading is simply Hardy's particularity about the social conditions of his fictional world. To take only one instance, Tess's father is a lifeholder of his cottage, and when he dies his lease dies with him, leaving his family homeless. It is as a direct result of this that Tess returns to Alec d'Urberville, is visited by Angel Clare, and fatally stabs her first seducer. To that extent the *dénouement* arises quite specifically from social conditions. But the action may be seen also in a larger context, historical rather than merely contemporary. Tess stands at a transitioanal point in the nineteenth century. Her education to the Sixth Standard at school sets her apart from her largely uneducated mother, but what she has lost in native wit she has not made up for in formal education. When she and her mother were together, 'the Jacobean and the Victorian ages were juxtaposed', says Hardy [p.61]. Given another twenty years

1

Tess would have been fully assimilated into a new century, but it is her misfortune to receive the worst.

The 'destruction of the peasantry' to which Kettle refers may also be seen symbolically. On one level Tess is the country girl seduced because she did not know 'there was danger in men', but on another she is the peasant sacrificed to a new age and new values. Kettle (1953) suggests that her mother's dressing her up before she is sent to 'seek kin' is a symbolic handing-over of Tess to the ruling class. Alec d'Urberville is not true aristocracy, but a representative of the new rulers, whose power is based not in the land, but in money acquired elsewhere. The peasant Durbeyfields are the victims of a movement in history, a whole social transformation, symbolised for Kettle by such incidents as the running-down of their lumbering horse and cart by the mail cart 'with its two noiseless wheels, speeding along these lanes like an arrow' [p.71] or Tess's forced labour on top of the steam threshing-machine. This latter incident is 'a symbol of the dehumanised relationships of the new capitalist farms' (p.52), and certainly Hardy's descriptions of the machine as a 'buzzing red glutton' whose faeces are straw, and which devours human labour as well as grain, would seem to bear out this view.

A modified sense of realism

The corollary of such a reading is that our sense of this novel as a traditionally realistic creation, held together by probability and a general sense of lifelikeness, has to be modified somewhat – hence Kettle's claim, already mentioned, that the work is a 'moral fable'. The more we read incidents and characters as representing something beyond themselves, as taking part in a demonstration of a thesis about history and society, the more we must read the whole novel as something schematised, representing meanings not conveyed simply by normal life processes – as a fable, indeed. In point of fact, Kettle, in conducting this argument, is killing more than one bird, since he feels the novel is relatively unconvincing at the level of simple realism, and by reading it symbolically he gives some *raison d'être* for the awkwardnesses of which he is aware.

Fundamentally these awkwardnesses are to do with improbability, and Kettle cites the well-known business of unlikely coincidence to support his case. Tess's letter to Angel unfortunately slips under the carpet; she has not the heart actually to visit Angel's parents, having walked all the way to their village, because she overhears her brothers-in-law talking about her. 'In the broader realm of probability', asks Kettle, 'is there really any adequate reason why Tess, at the end, should murder d'Urberville?' Not only are these matters of improbable ill luck, but, Kettle argues, they are also psychologically and socially improbable: 'Is not Tess, after all (admitting her superiority of sensitiveness), a good deal less shrewd and worldly-wise than a peasant girl of her age might naturally be assumed to be?' (p.54). Could she, for example, really have afforded the emotional luxury of simply abandoning her boots when they are found in the hedge by Mercy Chant and Angel's brothers [ch. 44]? Again, the dialogue is often unconvincing if read simply as 'psychological drama'. It does not ring true as an expression of an individual's feelings, but this is precisely Kettle's point. Hardy is stressing not individuality but typicality, a 'generalised human situation in history' (p.53). It is thus that we should understand Alec d'Urberville, who has all the manner of the conventional Victorian melodramatic villain, twirling his moustaches and addressing the girl he is to seduce as 'my Beauty'. Hardy is not simply setting up a cardboard figure because he cannot be bothered to do better, but presenting us with a stock caricature so that we may appreciate his typicality and 'understand better *why* the character of which he is a symbol did dominate a certain grade of Victorian entertainment and was enthusiastically hissed by the audience' (p.55). The idea that Hardy requires a supra-realistic reading is not, it should be said, confined to Kettle. It is, more or less, at the basis of all 'poetic' interpretations of the book. The special feature of Kettle's case is his suggestion that, by a distortion of the realistic texture, Hardy's eye is more clearly focused on social and historical concerns. Other critics, while agreeing with the sense of distortion, have a different conception of what comes into focus.

But social history may be a more complex matter

One of the major weaknesses, perhaps, of Kettle's position is that its general tendency is towards simplification. This may be felt even in the aspect which Kettle is most at pains to emphasise – the social and historical. A fellow Marxist critic, Raymond Williams, has suggested (1970) that Hardy's grasp of these elements is more complex than 'destruction of the English peasantry' would suggest. Williams's first point is that the word 'peasant' should be dropped altogether, since there were virtually no genuine peasants in England at that time. Instead there was a wide variety of country people – 'landowners, tenant farmers, dealers, craftsmen and labourers' – forming a social structure radically different from a peasantry. It is Williams's particular aim to disprove the suggestion that *Tess* shows us the impact of an alien urban world upon the 'timeless pattern' of English rural life. He sees the pressure as coming rather from within the rural community, and Hardy's interest (in many of his novels, not just *Tess*) as being in the character who has become 'in some degree separated from it yet who remain[s] by some tie of family inescapably involved' (p.102). As an illustration of this he cites Tess's ability to speak two languages:

> Mrs Durbeyfield habitually spoke the dialect; her daughter, who had passed the Sixth Standard in the National School under a London-trained mistress, spoke two languages; the dialect at home, more or less; ordinary English abroad and to persons of quality   [p.58]

Williams believes that Hardy's fascination with this situation derives particularly from the fact that he himself was describing a way of life with which he was 'closely yet uncertainly connected' (p.101). Williams's approach might be characterised as 'dynamic', in contrast to Kettle's rather static, schematised view of historical change. The former emphasises that the Wessex of *Tess* is a changing society, and one which is already very modern. He quotes Hardy himself as describing the district in the 1860s and 1870s as 'a modern Wessex of railways, the penny post, mowing and reaping machines, union workhouses, lucifer matches, labourers who could read and write, and National school children' (p.112). He therefore wishes to be far more realistic and pragmatic than Kettle about country life, defining Tess thus: 'Tess is not a peasant girl seduced by the squire; she is the daughter of a lifeholder and small dealer who is seduced by the son of a retired manufacturer' (p.114). He would like to get away from the rather sentimental vision of a changeless pastoral world, newly assaulted from without, and show a world where harsh economic processes of 'inheritance, capital, rent and trade' are acting in the 1890s as they had acted for centuries before to impose complex problems of change and adjustment upon rural communities. The complexities may be felt through what Williams says of the problems inherent in formally educating such a community: 'education is tied to social advancement within a class society, so that it is difficult, except by a bizarre personal demonsration, to hold both to education and to social solidarity' (p.104). Loyalties clash with desires and demands in a change which in superficial terms may be produced from outside (for example, the 1870 Education Act) but which is really part of a constant organic change. Society is never 'timeless'.

'Static' and 'dynamic' views of the novel

While this sense of 'dynamism' in the novel is attractive, it must be said in support of Kettle that a great many critics who have not perhaps supported his social interpretation have sensed in other ways something static about the work. Moreover, this staticness is not necessarily a weakness, but a thing which lends a largeness to the novel's concept of human destiny not fully apprehended by an interpretation so narrowly social as Williams's. Williams does, however, avoid one of the major weaknesses of the 'social' interpretation as we find it in Kettle. The latter, as we have seen, tends to take individuals rather as illustrations of general truths than as psychologically realistic figures. Williams will not accept this turning-away from essentially meaningful individuality: 'Yet they [the characters] are never merely illustrations of this change in a way of life. Each has a dominant personal history, which in psychological terms bears a direct relation to the social character of the change' (p.115).

Objections to the 'social' approach

In recognising this, Williams is avoiding, I feel, the criticism to which 'social' interpretations are most open. That is, put most basically, that to see the novel as anything other than a work of fundamental realism is to deny some of its richness and variety.

The criticism may not be so apparent in the symbolic interpretation of incidents such as the running-down of the Durbeyfield cart. We clearly feel that the moment is, before anything else, a real accidental misfortune. But when we consider people the case is very different. It is surely not enough to say that Tess, Angel and Alec (to go no further) are representatives of some generality such as 'the English peasantry', 'bourgeois values' and 'melodramatic villainy'. Even the most straightforward of these figures, Alec, is a more complex personality than this would suggest. He does not begin with a plan to seduce Tess; rather he is overtaken by an opportunity. He does not, and would not, abandon his victim, but on the contrary seems fatally drawn to her. Is this owing to love, passion, guilt or all of these things? His conversion to extreme evangelical Christianity and subsequent relapse into obsession with Tess are not so improbable as they might seem at first, if one is prepared to see them as the actions of a weak man who is obsessed by a woman in relation to whom he feels desire and guilt at the same time. Again, Kettle may be right in suggesting that a man of Angel's intelligence 'would not be quite so morally obtuse' as to see no affinity between his confession of a sexual lapse and Tess's, after she has confessed to him on their wedding-night. But Hardy is not thereby merely making a satiric point about something as general as 'male hypocrisy'. He is suggesting that Angel, like Alec (and perhaps like Tess also to some extent) is an extreme and irrational human being. The argument may apply, indeed, to the 'awkwardness' of the book as a whole. It could be claimed that Hardy introduced coincidence, oddity and improbability because he saw life as depending upon these elements at least as much as upon the more orderly concepts of historical and social change. Certainly, as far as 'character' is concerned we have only to look at what D.H. Lawrence made of the three-way relationship between Tess, Alec and Angel (see under '"Character" approaches') to see that Kettle is missing out a vital and dynamic human factor in wishing to deny individuality in favour of large symbols.

Is Tess a specifically female 'victim'?

While Williams is more subtle in his approach than Kettle, they have in common a basic assumption about the nature of the social aspect of Hardy's novel. Both see man as being the victim of some kind of historical change and economic pressure. If Tess is seen as being the main victim, for both critics she still remains either a symbol of her class, or only one of a large section of society. But Tess may also be seen as a victim as member of a quite different societal group – that of her own sex, subjected to the ill treatment and prejudices of a society whose values and assumptions are those of the opposite sex.

The fifth phase of *Tess* is called 'The Woman Pays' – a significant title in itself, I think. She is paying first for her seduction by a man who, from his personal beliefs and the prejudices of his class and age, felt himself licensed to take advantage of an innocent and pretty girl. Alec is not wicked, despite his 'stage-villain' appearance, and he genuinely wants to help Tess. But there is a coarseness underlying his whole attitude to her, from the condescending (and sexually suggestive) device of feeding her strawberries and decking her with flowers, to the exchange of her favours for his help in housing her family. Nothing could be more indicative of his feeling for her, and for women in general one presumes, than that he should ask her permission to smoke when she is a virgin, and after her 'fall' merely 'light up'.

Perhaps ultimately more painful for Tess is her treatment at the hands of the other man in her life. Angel Clare, sensitive and idealistic, would seem to be the complete opposite of Alec, but his behaviour when Tess tells her secret is all too clear a demonstration that chauvinism is not confined to the predatory male. In a sense, Angel's fault is that, while social conditioning teaches Alec that women are frail, and where possible to be taken advantage of, in the case of the parson's son it has convinced him that women are ideals of purity. When this ideal is punctured, it is too much for him to accept:

> 'But you do not forgive me?'
> 'O Tess, forgiveness does not apply to the case.
> You were one person; now you are another.' (p.298)

This simple duality emphasises the crushing duality of his own, and other men's, thinking on women, and it has already been reinforced by ironic references to Christianity's archetypal presentation of Woman – the Garden of Eden. When she and Clare walk alone together at Talbothays in the early morning, they feel 'isolation, as if they were Adam and Eve' [p.186]. Again, she looks at Angel 'as Eve at her second waking might have regarded Adam' [p.232]. But these seemingly innocent allusions contain a bitterly ironical reflection on the whole ethos of a Christian society. The concept of Eden is a part of the religious system which justifies the inhuman double standard of which Tess is a victim. Eden is the scene of the Fall, and Tess is a 'fallen woman'. On leaving Trantridge after her seduction, we are told that she had learned 'that the serpent hisses where the sweet birds sing' [p.123]. *Her* serpent-betrayer was a man, but in the Christian myth the serpent corrupted Eve, who then passed her corruption to Adam. It is notable that, when Clare sees her at a moment of intense sensuousness, as she stretches and yawns langorously, he sees 'the red interior of her mouth as if it had been a snake's' [p.231]. But her serpent image is ironic. She is not a temptress, being unaware of Angel's presence; yet unconsciously her beauty is felt as a seductive, almost corrosive, power over both Clare and Alec. Alec in particular is inclined to see himself as a victim of Tess's attractions, and more generally she finds herself a victim of her own beauty, until eventually she has to clip her eyebrows and make herself as ugly as possible in order to avoid the undesired attentions of men on the road.

'Society' may imply a fundamentally unnatural 'civilisation'

Such a perversion of what is natural and beautiful leads us to the last and largest sense in which the problems of *Tess* may be seen as social ones. Hitherto we have taken 'society' in a rather particular and concrete way – customs, history, economics. But 'society' implies also, in a general sense, 'civilisation' – all those things which we believe mark off man from animals in 'wild nature'. And taken in this sense there would seem to be a duality maintained by Hardy between this 'civilisation' and the natural, much to the detriment of the former. As I have already suggested, the main repository of the natural is Tess herself, although ironically she fails to see this. Her mother is almost a personification of amoral, unchanging acceptance of the natural way of things. She accepts Tess's pregnancy with the

resigned "Tis nater, after all and what do please God!' [p.131].
And where the mother's natural sexual cunning would have
made her conceal the past from Clare, the daughter puts her
trust in a professed emancipation before the time is ripe for its
practice. Again, as with the problems of sexual morality,
Christianity appears to embody the conventional and
unnatural, a function particularly seen in Tess's attitude to her
baby. As she lies in bed, realising the child is dying, she is
tormented by fears which are peculiarly poignant because of
the grotesque imagery, combining eternal torment with the
domestic scene:

> She thought of the child consigned to the nethermost corner
> of hell, as its double doom for lack of baptism and lack of
> legitimacy; saw the arch-fiend tossing it with his
> three-pronged fork, like the one they used for heating the
> oven on baking days . . . [p.143]

Her fears are induced by a cruelly twisted and unnatural
theological system, and the priest she consults about the baby's
burial does little to alleviate her fears by his relentless insistence
(at first at least) on the letter of 'God's law'. Hardy puts the
final seal on his case against Christianity's unnatural cruelty
when he tells that the child was buried 'in that shabby corner of
God's allotment where He lets the nettles grow, and where all
unbaptized infants, notorious drunkards, suicides, and others
of the conjecturally damned are laid'. [p.148]

Angel Clare also is betrayed by a forced, unnatural ethos.
Yielding to the spontaneous impulse of a moment, he stays
behind to dance with the village girls, and sees Tess, although
he does not dance with her. Had the naturalness of that
symbolic moment been maintained, it would have been better
for himself and Tess, but he follows the call of his brothers,
eager to get through another chapter of *A Counterblast to
Agnosticism*. And it is Angel's misfortune to be unable to yield to
what is natural in his wife until it is too late, corrupted as he is
by false values. He thinks his views are 'advanced' compared to
those of his brothers and his father, but they are a superficial
varnish. His practical view of the world in the matter of one
whom he claims to love is no more charitable than theirs, and
probably less so in the case of his parents. When Tess first tells

him her secret, he replies to her cry, 'I will obey you like your wretched slave, even if it is to lie down and die', with a remark which is not merely cruel, but which employs the devious, intellectual device of irony, a device 'the charms of [whose] subtlety passed by her unappreciated': 'You are very good. But it strikes me that there is a want of harmony between your present mood of self-sacrifice and your past mood of self-preservation' [p.300]. The famous scene in which, sleepwalking, he carries Tess in his arms and places her in a sarcophagus suggests the conflicts and repressions in his own mind. It is only in sleep that he can use terms of endearment to her – 'My poor, poor Tess' [p.318]. Laying her in the tomb symbolises not only the fact that she is dead to him, but perhaps also his need to sacrifice her for his unnatural ideals.

The natural–unnatural polarity is reinforced throughout the book by numerous images in which the hand of man is seen to be distorting the natural or inanimate world. An 'old grey wall' receives the foreboding words of society and religion, 'THOU SHALT, NOT, COMMIT –' 'with a strange and unwonted mien, as if distressed at duties it had never before been called upon to perform', [p.129]. The willows at Talbothays, 'tortured out of their natural shape by incessant choppings, become spiny-haired monsters' [p.241]. The madness and depraved cruelty of civilisation are suggested in the description of the hunters who have destroyed birds in the copse where the hunted Tess lies all night:

> She had been told that, rough and brutal as they seemed just then, they were not like this all the year round, but were, in fact, quite civil persons save during certain weeks of autumn and winter, when, like the inhabitants of the Malay Peninsula, they ran amuck, and made it their purpose to destroy life –   [p.352]

By contrast we see the humanity and strength of Tess as she kills the birds 'tenderly'.

The opposition between natural and 'forced' was observed in *Tess* as long ago as 1894 by Lionel Johnson in *The Art of Thomas Hardy*. Johnson is inclined to quarrel with Hardy over the question of what 'Nature' is, feeling that the novelist has not formed a clear conception of what he means by the term: 'Mr

Hardy juggles with 'Nature': now she is cruel, which is a reproach to divine justice; now she is kindly, whereas society is harsh' (p.233). This is a crucial example of what a number of critics have felt to be a typical confusion in the novel. It is a confusion particularly associated with *causes* in *Tess,* and we shall return to the matter in the 'Appraisal' part of the book.

'Character' approaches

Social interpretations of novels tend to play down the importance of the individual, who is often seen as at best expressing historical tendencies, and at worst as simply the victim of forces beyond his or her control. In this section I shall be discussing views of Tess which centre on 'character' in its own right – the individual as an agent of his own destiny and standing alone as an expression of the meaning of the work of art.

The degree of control exercised by human beings is an important question in *Tess,* and I shall begin by presenting a viewpoint which sees the heroine as to some extent responsible by her failings for her own downfall, and oppose this interpretation with one which holds her up as a static figure, containing and expressing a human ideal.

Is Tess morally responsible for her own fate?

The first of these arguments is expressed most interestingly by Roy Morrell in his book *Thomas Hardy, The Will and the Way* (1965). His study focuses on Tess herself, but she is not the only figure whom we might wish to censure as showing some weakness of character. The folly, ignorance and superstition of her parents are things of which Tess herself is well aware. If it had not been for her father's obstinate clinging to the supposed past glories of his family (and his attendant drunkenness) much of Tess's painful future might have been averted. And Angel Clare can hardly be spared some censure for his selfishness, and obtuseness to the real virtues of his wife. But Morrell is concerned with a larger question than that suggested by localised failures of moral fibre. His belief that character determines the meaning of the novel is based upon seeing possibility where other critics, he feels, have seen determinism.

Tess of the D'Urbervilles turns, for Morrell, upon choices – choices whether to commit oneself or not. The part played by character in this is that Tess (for example) does not have the moral strength to make the choice she knows she ought. Rejecting the idea that a 'proleptic' image of the gallows made by a knife and fork projects Tess's eventual and inevitable fate, Morrell says,

> In the three hundred pages of that novel between the 'proleptic' image and the gallows (no wonder the reader is not struck by it on first reading!) the whole rhythm and tension of our interest is controlled by the reprieves, the rallies, the second chances; by our sense of what might, even at a late stage, be done to prevent the disaster.   (p.18)

In support of this he can cite a number of turning-points in the story at which the choice the character makes is crucial to his or her destiny. Many times Tess is prompted to confess to Angel. Fearing to tell him, she writes a letter, only to recover it after it has inadvertently slipped under the mat. Her deep-seated desire not to tell is suggested in her reaction to this unfortunate discovery: 'The incident of the misplaced letter she had jumped at as if it prevented a confession; but she knew in her conscience that it need not; there was still time' [p.277]. We are told by Hardy that Tess would have been spared all her later sufferings had she seen Angel's parents, but she turns back when almost on their doorstep, lacking the final resolution required. Clare says that, if Tess had told him of his sleepwalking, 'it might have prevented much misunderstanding and woe' (p.480). Clare himself is 'within a featherweight's turn' of going back to Tess when Izz Huett tells him of his wife's love [ch. 40]. All these points may be seen as crucial, but, where many critics would see them as reinforcing a sense of fatal inevitability, Morrell believes they show that things *might* have been altered, given greater determination in the characters.

Morrell's argument is particularly centred on trying to indicate how far Tess fell short of her 'considerable potentialities'. Tess, he says, 'chooses not to choose' rather than makes bad choices. So she slides into marriage under Clare's importunities, as she had acquiesced in the demands of Alec. She knows she *should* be frank with Clare, but avoids deciding to be so. In place of decision Tess is content to drift in an almost dreamlike state from situation to situation in her life. In this way she can see herself as victim, whether of other people or of 'the way things are'. This dreamlike state would seem to be taken more or less literally by Hardy, who several times alludes to her ability to dissociate her mind from her body. Angel realises, when he finds her living at Sandbourne with Alec, 'that his original Tess had spiritually ceased to recognize the body before him as hers – allowing it to drift, like a corpse upon the current, in a direction dissociated from its living will' [p.467]. Angel himself, of course, has preferred dreams to reality – in his case, romantic dreams of the perfect woman in an idyllic setting. These dreams are sadly shattered by a reality he cannot face. And Tess's parents also are misled by visions – one of family greatness, the other of her daughter's being elevated into a lady by their 'cousin'.

For Morrell, Hardy's characters, whatever they may feel, are not the slaves of blind chance, let alone Fate. If 'things', 'events' are not left to themselves, but moulded by the will of determined human beings decided on a certain course of action, the human beings will not be hurt. Only those, such as Tess, who 'choose not to choose', who will not find the will to make a way, are lost. Against those who would say that the series of missed chances only emphasises the inevitability of the novel's tragic outcome, Morrell would argue that these are 'near-misses' which bring out how possible it was for the character to have pressed on and made the *possible* good *actual*. He can also cite instances of determined characters who, by action, would seem to have averted an 'inevitable' disaster. Such is Gabriel Oak, in *Far from the Madding Crowd*, who saves the corn ricks from storm, despite omens of disaster. In the same novel, when Sergeant Troy has decided that Fate, in ruining Fanny Robin's grave, has shown itself his enemy, the Sergeant gives up for ever, while Oak, with Bathsheba's assistance, repairs the grave, and the 'gurgoyle' which had caused the damage. Morrell's instances, however, are not drawn from *Tess*, and it might be suggested that this reinforces the sense of helplessness which many people feel has distinguished the heroine. Hardy's hints of what might have been never are shown as realities, and it could be said that the emphasis on the hairs-breadth difference between 'was' and 'might' only ironically reveals the yawning gap between the two.

Morrell's conception of the part character plays in *Tess* is based on an externalised view of personality, and on the centrality of moral action in the form of conscious choice. Such an interpretation is open to the individual's own preferences in interpreting human motivation. While Morrell sees Tess's turning-back from her parents-in-law's door as 'simple cowardice' (p.98) rather than scrupulosity arising from her sensitivity, another reader might espouse her cause by citing many instances of her superior moral qualities, most notably in the central act of telling her secret to Clare. Her mother's cunning had counselled silence, but Tess shows greater honesty and courage (after all, despite the procrastination, she *does* eventually tell). It is an act of self-commitment she perhaps need never have carried out.

Tess's virtues

There are clearly episodes which show Tess to have a number of positive virtues, and to be fair to Morrell it must be admitted that he calls her a 'mixed' character. But his general tendency is to see moral negatives in her personality as ultimately defining what her fate will be. As a contrast we may turn to Irving Howe, a critic who also sees Tess's character as central to the novel's meaning, but in a far more positive sense than Morrell. In fact Howe's interpretation (1966) shows the ambiguity inherent in this 'externalised' approach to character, since he also relies heavily on the concept of 'possibility'. But, while for Morrell this is potential unrealised and therefore morally reprehensible, Howe sees the figure of Tess as representing all that could be, and what happens to her as signifying all that life too often becomes. Yet she signifies these things by being a human being – a woman made real. The characteristics that he focuses on are essentially positive ones, despite the strong element of the painful and pessimistic Howe acknowledges finding in the book. So he emphasises her resilience, seen in her 'high spirits', her energy and joy, and those characteristics he sees as particularly womanly – affection, trust, the faculties of survival and suffering. He remarks on her endless variety: 'She can flirt, she can listen, she can sympathise, she can work with her hands' (p.131). He sees her not only as sensitive but also as clear-headed, citing her response to the vicar who refuses her child Christian burial: '"Then I don't like you!" she burst out, "and I'll never come to your church no more!"' (p.147). This, says Howe, is not mere feminine illogicality but the rejection of a man of God who can so heartlessly deprive another human being of comfort.

The danger of losing the individual in her virtues

Despite his insistence that it is in Tess as a human being that we apprehend all this, it must be recognised that Howe's interpretation leads us *through* that human individuality to feel certain general qualities. She 'embodies a moral poise beyond the reach of most morality (p.130). She is 'human life stretched and racked, yet forever springing back to renewal' (ibid.). This is clearly a very different idea of 'character' from Morrell's. The Tess that Morrell sees is one essentially *acting* in time and place, brought constantly to crossroads in a life which is defined by moral choices. Finally he sees her as inadequate to life's challenge, but it is not enough simply to contrast this with Howe's version and say that Howe sees her as perfectly adequate. To him she is more than this, since he sees her in another dimension. Other characters plot, social setting and ideas are not dynamic testing-devices, says Howe, but subordinate accessories to the figure of Tess. The plot in isolation is 'a paltry thing, a mere scraping together of bits and pieces from popular melodrama' (p.112). The secondary figures are useful, but 'finally they are little more than accessories, whose task is not so much to draw attention in their own right as to heighten the reality of Tess' (p.131).

Howe's interpretation is notable for its lack of specific illustration, and, while one must applaud his wholehearted celebration of the positive in Tess, his tendency is to turn the novel into a paean on life's potentialities so generalised that on almost any page one might find a particular instance which would undermine his confident rhetoric. Nevertheless, Howe is important as representing an extreme statement of one side of an argument about the nature of the whole novel as it is manifested in 'character'. His approach is intensely 'affective'. However dynamic in various specific situations Tess may be, ultimately we feel her as a static representative of a cluster of human virtues. The whole of the novel is ultimately geared to presenting *her*. Morrell, at the opposite pole, sees character (Tess's and others') as being a vitally causative matter, interacting with circumstances to produce a particular outcome.

A more pragmatic compromise

We do not, perhaps, have to espouse either of these extreme views. Bejamin Sankey (1965) adopts what might be termed a 'pragmatic' interpretation of Tess's character. For him 'Tess represents the best that human nature has to offer' (p.165). She is not absolutely morally reprehensible, nor a paragon of human possibility. When the family's horse is run down, the causes are multiple – her father's drunkenness, her mother's procrastination, Tess's drowsiness. The death itself leads to Tess's sense of guilt, and hence to her acquiescence in her mother's plan and so to her seduction. We can see this as a logical sequence, but Tess cannot. She acts from moment to moment as best she can in a complex and changing situation. There is no great choice for Tess on which the whole of her fate depends. It is made up from a series of 'minor and unrelated events' (p.96), and, while she cannot be exonerated, her ultimate death cannot be said to be directly related to moments which presented themselves to Tess at the time as diffuse and unrelated. Sankey's interpretation is ultimately moral, but only in so far as it sees the context of the whole story as moral. Hardy's project was 'an attempt to confront a sensitive and well-meaning person, equipped with a decent set of values, with a world which makes no special allowances for those values' (p.98). It is clearly more difficult to blame Tess in these circumstances than in the view presented by Morrell.

The 'subconscious' interpretation of character

All these versions of a 'character'-based approach to *Tess* are more or less moral in their assumptions. The personality is a matter of externalised, analysable features, to be measured by a moral code which is related in turn to the total significance of the work of art. Howe is the least strictly moral, but even he is assessing Tess basically by her conscious self. When, as in the case of her resilience, the quality is unself-conscious, he assesses it as a virtue. But there is a quite different approach to character, which sees the human being driven at least as much by his subscious as by his conscious self, and *Tess* seems to be a novel which is quite amenable to such an interpretation. Clearly we are none of us sane, rational creatures all the time, living by rule and calculation. We are driven by wants, needs, desires and hates, by those darker forces which modern psychology has drawn into the open, though artists such as Hardy had instinctively felt their presence long before.

One of the greatest virtues of such an approach is that it can confront the problem of sex as it is manifested in *Tess of the d'Urbervilles* without being influenced by prior assumptions about morality, society and other distortions. The problem for the critic who takes this line is that the evidence in the text is often rather thin, compared with that for more conventional interpretations. He may end with a view of the characters' relationships and motivation which at first sight seems in direct opposition to the manifest evidence. The critic must catch the imagination of his reader from the start, so that the latter can see the whole text in a completely new light, otherwise a 'subconscious' approach may seem simply perverse. Its greatest exponent as regards *Tess,* and indeed all Hardy's novels, has been D. H. Lawrence (1936), whose distinctive style, while it can make understanding difficult, must be taken as part of the whole interpretation, since I think it is the means by which Lawrence signals that he is giving what amounts to a highly individual *version* of *Tess.*

The distinctiveness of the writing extends to Lawrence's special use of words. He speaks, for example, of 'aristocracy' in both Tess and Alec, clearly not meaning high birth, but referring to a deep personality characteristic. In Tess it is a kind of 'insouciance' – knowing herself to *be* herself and no other person. She respects other people's right to be, and does not seek to change or affect another person in any way. Unfortunately for her, the two men in her life cannot respect *her* 'right to be'. Both cannot avoid involving themselves with her in some way which uses her personality, or what they make of it. Alec, says Lawrence, adheres to Tess 'like a parasite'. He is only a fragmentary man in himself, but he needs something he can get from Tess, which Lawrence calls 'the deep impulse'. He perhaps means something like 'reason for existence' by this phrase. But this puts Alec in a specially close relationship with Tess, because he can reach into the deepest recesses of a woman. It is perhaps this 'rare quality' in Alec which Lawrence characterises as 'aristocratic'. He is the complete opposite of Angel Clare, for whom the female in himself – that is, the body and the senses – is detestable. Angel has reacted against the Christian principle which would deny the body, but only so far, and, while he must accept and acknowledge the woman, his ascetic self and his deeper, subconscious self are waging a battle. Generations of Christian training have taught Clare that man is the exclusive whole of life, but in seeking Tess he has to accept femaleness too, and this is terribly painful for him. In both Clare and Alec, says Lawrence, 'there is good stuff gone wrong' (p.487). The former represents the Cavalier idea, celebrating woman as the only good; the latter the Puritan idea, 'the Male Principle, of Abstraction, of Good, of Public Good, of the Community' (ibid.). Inevitably Angel and Alec mutually destroy the woman they both loved.

Lawrence's interpretation very distinctive

Beneath the rhetoric Lawrence is perhaps saying some rather traditional things. He sees the novel as tragic, and Tess as a victim. In speaking of 'good' 'gone wrong' he is invoking *some* kind of moral judgement. 'Aristocracy' does, for him, involve a matter of generations of breeding. Nevertheless, Lawrence represents one of the most unusual approaches to the novel, which, while it has been grouped under the heading 'character', almost deserves to belong to a group of its own. For his sense of tragic inevitability has its roots in psychological types who are perhaps archetypes; his moral categories refer to instinctual tendencies for which the characters cannot be praised or blamed, and the word 'aristocrat' is not used socially, or even biologically, so much as mystically, to describe the essential 'selfness' as man and woman of Alec and Tess.

Other aspects of the subconscious are viable interpretations

If the reader once accepts that overt causes and motivation may not be the whole story of *Tess,* he may feel that there are other ways than Lawrence's of reading the subconscious, 'unacknowledged' side of character. Morrell suggests that Tess brings about her own destruction to some extent by a failure of moral nerve at certain crucial moments. His assumption is that she would presumably rather *not* hve brought her fate upon herself. Yet it is not wildly improbable to suggest that there is a self-destructive, fatalistic side to Tess which may deliberately court persecution, mistreatment and rejection. When she is working on the ricks at farmer Groby's, Tess, persecuted by the attentions of Alec d'Urberville, strikes him across the mouth with her heavy gauntlet, making his lips bleed:

> She too had sprung up, but she sank down again.
> 'Now, punish me!' she said, turning up her eyes to him with the hopeless defiance of the sparrow's gaze before its captor twists its neck. 'Whip me, crush me; you need not mind those people under the rick! I shall not cry out. Once victim, always victim – that's the law!'   [p.411]

The language here is at least masochistic, and the outburst ends with a pronouncement which seems decidedly fatalistic. Many readers have commented on Tess's passivity, but could it perhaps be that 'Do what you like with me, mother' [p.89] is something more positive than passivity – that subconsciously she actively seeks the role of victim? Certainly her pronouncements on the state of the world, before any particular misfortune other than her birth has befallen her, suggest a somewhat gloomy view of the human condition:

> 'Did you say the stars were worlds, Tess?'
> 'Yes.'
> 'All like ours?'
> 'I don't know; but I think so. They sometimes seem to be like the apples on our stubbard-tree. Most of them splendid and sound – a few blighted.'
> 'Which do we live on – a splendid one or a blighted one?'
> 'A blighted one.'   [pp. 69–70]

This is her reaction to what she sees of life in her own family, and the interpretation I am here advancing can be linked to a sense of decay of which, as we saw in the Introduction, Hardy himself was very conscious. If one believes subconsciously that one is at the end of a declining race, then there is a possibility that one will instinctively turn to meet that decline, let it frame one's destiny, and even welcome it. If she is masochistic in her dealings with Alec, Tess shows at times an almost dog-like devotion to Clare, and seems to welcome chances of suffering and self-sacrifice. When her boots are taken by Mercy Chant, she indulges herself with the following reflection: "'Ah!" she said, still sighing in pity of herself, "*they* didn't know that I wore those over the roughest part of the road to save these pretty ones he bought for me – no – they did not know it!'" [p.377]. And one wonders how far her refusal to ask for them or to knock at her father-in-law's door is the result of timidity, and how far of a need to see herself victimised. Perhaps to some extent she creates her own role, and then acts it out. If this seems a hard judgement, we might consider that Tess is not alone among characters in Hardy novels who could be seen as having a self-destructive urge. Farmer Boldwood, in *Far from the Madding Crowd*, Giles Winterbourne and Marty South in *The Woodlanders*, Clym Yeobright and Eustacia Vye in *The Return of the Native*, and Michael Henchard, the Mayor of Casterbridge, all seem, in differing degrees admittedly, to show some perverse desire for self-sacrifice or self-immolation. Hardy is also very frequently concerned with characters who show almost pathological extremes of temperament, and in the case of a figure such as Alec d'Urberville this extremeness could well be seen to be the central fact about him. He flies from sensuality to extreme religiosity and back again, with no in-between stages. Angel Clare, too, has no life between elevation of Tess as an embodiment of purity, and total rejection of her as an entirely different woman. There is, in short, a manic, extreme quality in many of Hardy's novels which is manifest in lurid scenes and incidents, in grotesque coincidences and, most of all perhaps, in personality.

But the conscious self is also crucial to Hardy

Yet, before we are completely seduced by the 'subconscious' view of character, it would be well to remember that Tess's conscious self is emphasised on many occasions by Hardy. The section in which she moves from her home to Talbothays Dairy after the death of her baby is entitled 'The Rally', and clearly this means that Tess herself is to be seen as recovering from her setback, determinedly building up her life, and finding new love. For every moment of self-abasement before Clare, there is at least one clearsighted condemnation of his cruelty by Tess. She has a determination to survive, seen in its lowest form in her dogged working on through the winter at Flintcomb-Ash, and at its highest when she contemplates suicide as Angel, sleepwalking, carries her across a river (she rejects the idea because he would drown too). I have already mentioned her wringing the necks of the dying game-birds. At the sane time as she does this tough and compassionate act she upbraids herself:

'Poor darlings – to suppose myself the most miserable being on earth in the sight o' such misery as yours!' she exclaimed, her tears running down as she killed the birds tenderly. 'And not a twinge of bodily pain about me! I be not mangled, and I be not bleeding; and I have two hands to feed and clothe me.'   [p.353]

It is hard to see the woman who can say such a thing as a self-destroyer; or, if we *are* to adopt this stance, such a passage must modify the interpretation considerably.

'Ideas' approaches

When considering Hardy as a 'novelist of ideas' we must immediately be aware of the way in which categories such as those I have established in this book for ease of discussion and understanding are arbitrary, and may overlap each other. In a sense, all that I have written of so far is a matter of 'ideas' – ideas of character, moral responsibility, the place of the subconscious, how society evolves and its relation to the individual, the opposition between 'Nature' and 'civilisation'. This last 'idea' is in fact one to be mentioned in this section, but with a different emphasis. For the 'ideas' to be discussed here are those which may be vaguely termed 'philosophical'. They are the largest issues, of man's destiny, the existence of God, the meaning or lack of meaning in life, and, most particularly, the way in which a specific age finds itself facing these eternal problems.

The problem of Hardy's 'intrusive voice'

Apart from his language, it is as a propagator of ideas that Hardy has been most heavily criticised. Readers have tended to look at isolated comments in Hardy's own 'voice' in the novels and condemn them as trite and commonplace. Lionel Johnson, in his study of Hardy already cited, said he could not rank this novel as high as some of Hardy's previous works precisely because the 'insinuated argument' in the author's own voice seemed more than usually intrusive:

> Its spirit is nothing new, for all Mr Hardy's books proceed from the same range of thought: but none of them show quite this irritability of casual comment: this refusal to let the facts of the story convey their own moral, without the help of epigrammatic hints. At times, they read like quaint, modern imitations of those marginal glosses, which adorn the *Pilgrim's Progress* and the *Ancient Mariner:* 'Here Tess illustrateth the falling out betwixt Nature and Society', or, 'In this place did Angel mock at Giant Calvinist, for that he taught an untenable redemptive theolatry.'   (p.219)

Tess is notorious for a sentence upon which a whole theory of Hardy's 'beliefs' has been based: '"Justice" was done, and the President of the Immortals, in Aeschylean phrase, had ended his sport with Tess' [p.489]. Innumerable readers have seen here (despite Hardy's vehement denials) a picture of the Cosmos dominated by some all-too-tangible figure who, having decided Tess's path by closing off various possible exits with his finger, as it were, eventually squashes her like a fly that he is tired of tormenting. But, when we take into account the words 'in Aeschylean phrase', this view must surely be modified. First, 'the President of the Immortals' *is*, according to Hardy, an Aeschylean phrase, being a literal translation from the Greek dramatist. More importantly, it stands as a modifier of the term 'President of the Immortals'. Hardy's implication, I think, is that in the age of Aeschylus such an idea would be invoked to explain what has always been, and still is, inexplicable: why mankind should find itself tormented and destroyed for no apparent purpose or reason. But, we must understand, the Aeschylean explanation *is* of and for another age. It must not be taken to imply that Hardy still accepts such an explanation in the nineteenth century. What does remain is the problem, and, in the acute form in which it presented itself to the Victorians, it is probably the central 'idea' which Hardy was concerned with in his later novels.

David J. De Laura (1967) has called this compound of problem, idea and feeling 'the ache of modernism', a phrase drawn from *Tess* itself, and which Hardy glosses as 'feelings which might almost have been called those of the age' [p.180]. Clare immediately reflects that 'advanced ideas are really in great part but the latest fashion in definition': 'a more accurate expression, by words in *logy* and *ism*, of sensations which men and women have vaguely grasped for centuries' [ibid.]. This could suggest that Hardy was not concerned particularly with the specific ideas of his own age. Such was the belief of Ian Gregor when he wrote, in a comment quoted by De Laura, that 'If Hardy is predominantly a philosophical novelist, then it is remarkable how little gets into the fiction of such dominant nineteenth-century intellectual concerns as the clash between science and faith, the maintenance of ethics without religion' (p.380). De Laura maintains, however, that Hardy *was* expressing in *Tess* versions of certain ideas which had preoccupied the minds of leading thinkers in the mid-Victorian era.

The influence of Arnold

The particular writer to whom, according to De Laura, Hardy was specially indebted for his 'anatomy of the modern condition' is Matthew Arnold. Arnold had, in his early poetry, defined the 'emotional price of modernism' (Ibid). In this context 'modernism' means an increasing awareness of and reliance on a rational and scientific view of man. Comforted by a belief in a Christian God of love, a sense of Providence and a trust in personal immortality and salvation of the soul, it was possible for human beings to face the world with some degree of confidence, even though that world might seem narrowly bounded. To doubt or even completely abandon Christianity, and to espouse biology, mechanics and Darwinism in its place, was in one sense a liberation. Morally there was no longer any need to feel guilt (though obviously men did not stop feeling guilt). Intellectually the whole universe seemed suddenly more open. Unhampered by a 'First Cause' or a 'Divine Plan', the possibilities of life seemed as wide as man's imagination. But freedom has its price, and it is precisely this cost which Arnold defined, and which Hardy took up as his major theme.

The most striking price that the Victorian had to pay for his freedom was precisely the lack of that security from which he felt himself to be liberated. De Laura calls it 'the sense of psychic dislocation and alienation, of wandering in an unmapped no man's land "between two worlds"' (pp.380-1). Arnold had suggested some ways of grappling with this new situation *intellectually*, but for Hardy he had 'fatally compromised' himself in the 1870s by adopting a position which was 'metaphysically agnostic but emotionally and morally traditional and "Christian"' (p.381). In other words, Arnold was divided between an 'advanced' view of the nature of things, in which men could not subscribe to a faith in God or know with any certainty what their lives meant, and an irrational but understandable desire to cling to past comforts, emotionally and morally. These comforts gave personal reassurance, and a feeling that some stability was being maintained. Those who followed this attempt at compromise between old and new were, Hardy felt, destined to do so at great cost to their happiness.

The obvious example of this Arnoldian type in *Tess of the d'Urbervilles* is Angel Clare. The first words Hardy uses to describe him when he reappears in Tess's life at Talbothays suggest a person who has lost his way in life: 'Nevertheless, something nebulous, preoccupied, vague, in his bearing and regard, marked him as one who probably had no very definite aim or concern about his material future' [p.169]. Between himself and his father there is such a difference in age that there seems 'almost a missing generation' [ibid.] – clearly a metaphor for the divide between the old, Low Church parson, thoroughly devout, and his comparatively free-thinking youngest son. The stability and security of the *spiritual* life he could have inherited from his father is suggested by the unchanging pattern of his family's social destiny. Both his brothers have gone to Cambridge, and both are ordained. Clare wishes to strike out for himself. He cannot believe in the literal resurrection of Christ, so cannot be ordained, and turns instead to farming, as a vocation which will 'afford an independence without the sacrifice of what he valued even more than a competency – intellectual liberty' [p.172].

As we know, of course, his vaunted intellectual liberty is not sufficient to give him freedom from the moral and emotional assumptions he has inherited. He is a man completely split in two, as is demonstrated by his being 'nearly entrapped by a woman much older than himself' when he was in London. This escapade was the 'balance', says Hardy, to the 'austerities' of his intellectual pretensions [ibid.]. The disastrous consequence of this is that he is appalled at the real expression of his free-thinking in practical, human terms – namely, the fact that Tess has been seduced and has had an illegitimate child. The 'ache of modernism' is manifested for him as a painful revelation that the world is not as ideal as he would have it. De Laura sees Angel as seeking some form of 'Hellenism' – a vaguely Ancient Greek way of life which is essentially natural, spontaneous and pagan, by contrast with the Christian way. He remarks in a fit of annoyance to his father on one occasion, 'that it might have resulted far better for mankind if Greece had been the source of the religion of modern civilization, and not Palestine' [p.218]. But Angel cannot pursue the purity of the intellectual *idea* in the face of the real emotional demands of his nature, which are natural but are perverted by his own inherited narrowness of vision:

> This division between intellectual commitment and high ethical resolve on the one hand (a mid-Victorian heritage), and the experience of paralysis of will and emotion in the late nineteenth-century situation on the other, is the structure of the actual 'modern' dilemma faced by Hardy's latter-day heroes.   (De Laura, p.397).

The world without Providence

Two other themes are cited by De Laura as being crucial to Hardy's presentation of 'modernism'. First there is the rootlessness, the sense of drift in a world without Providence.

References to this are to be found throughout the novel, perhaps the most famous being the authorial comment on Tess's original seduction:

> But, might some say, where was Tess's guardian angel? where was the providence of her simple faith? Perhaps, like that other god of whom the ironical Tishbite spoke, he was talking, or he was pursuing, or he was in a journey, or he was sleeping and not to be awaked. [p.119]

As with the 'Aeschylean phrase', we must be wary of taking this passage as a suggestion on Hardy's part that there is some malign or indifferent actual presence overlooking Tess. The point of the rather heavy irony is that there is *no* presence, no Providence. We may also recall Tess's explanation to her younger brother Abraham that they live on a planet blighted like some of the apples on the stubbard tree. The analogy of heavenly bodies with apples on a tree is significant, because it reduces that which had always been seen as the province of God's particular and certain care to objects indifferently sound or blighted, purely according to chance.

Hardy and Christianity

De Laura's third theme is the direct condemnation of Christianity by Hardy, particularly as it is manifested in the practices of the late-nineteenth-century Church. It is here that the most bitterly ironic of Hardy's feelings are manifested, usually by way of direct authorial commentary. At Tess's seduction there might have been a possibility of some retribution 'lurking in the present catastrophe'; 'But though to visit the sins of the fathers upon the children may be a morality good enough for divinities, it is scorned by average human nature; and it therefore does not mend the matter' [p.119]. The vicar who hears of Tess's 'home baptism' is described as 'Having the natural feelings of a tradesman at finding that a job he should have been called in for had been unskilfully botched by his customers among themselves . . .' [p.147].

Yet again, care is needed in reading such passages. The somewhat sneering attack is crude enough, but Hardy is attacking dogma and the ridiculous paraphernalia of faith as he saw it, rather than the sincere practice of Christianity. The Reverend Mr Clare is treated with considerable sympathy. He and his wife are something of the type of primitive Christianity, simple, honest and charitable. They would have taken Tess in when their son's 'advanced' ideas had rejected her. Hardy's attitude to Christianity would seem to be yet another version of the 'natural' as opposed to 'civilised' – in this case the good-hearted and spontaneous *versus* the dogmatic and narrow. But, if anything, his greatest disapproval is reserved, as De Laura sees it, for 'neo-Christianity': the kind of unhappy compromise between old and new we have seen in Angel Clare.

What part do 'ideas' play in the work of art?

There is a crucial question still to be asked with regard to what I have called the 'ideas' approach to *Tess*. We may be convinced that Hardy has embodied certain ideas in his novel, and we may trace these ideas to their sources in certain nineteenth-century thinkers, but, if they are to amount to a coherent critical attitude, it must be established what role they play in the full meaning of the book as a work of art. How central are they, and are they more than 'sideswipes' or localised social issues of the 1890s? I mention these latter possibilities because they undoubtedly play some part in Hardy's concern with ideas, and not merely in *Tess*. In more than one of his novels, for example, he attacks the difficulty his society encountered in obtaining a divorce. While there is perhaps nothing quite so specific as this in *Tess*, we may ask whether his aim with regard to ideas is didactic or satiric in some sense. De Laura believes that 'Tess, especially, becomes a demand for greater honesty in confronting (to use Arnold's own youthful phrase) "the modern situation in its true *blankness* and *barrenness*, and unpoetryless-ness"' (p.382). Could the call for honesty also encompass a satiric attack on the sexual double standards of his day? This would be particularly apparent in Clare's rejection of Tess, but is also generally felt in the role played by Tess in relation to the men who surround her.

Alternatively, does the novel work as an animation of ideas? Has Hardy begun with the intention of displaying, say, the crisis of conscience in England in the last quarter of the nineteenth century and then fleshed out his idea in the form of a novel whose action and people body forth this problem? I have to say that I find neither of these answers very satisfying. There clearly are didactic elements in *Tess*, but they must surely be seen as somewhat peripheral to the final sense of the novel's force, which is tragic. And, while we are most certainly aware of the metaphysical problem of living in England in the 1890s – 'the ache of modernism' – it would seem perverse to see this as the *raison d'être* of the whole novel. If this were so we would have to accept that the final meaning of the book was the presentation of a problem for the reader's contemplation. A further result of such a stance would be to throw the weight of the book's meaning very heavily onto Angel Clare, as the figure most aware of this problem, and the best-informed on the subject. Both these necessary considerations must surely be distortions of a book which lives, finally, not through its own intellectual attainments, nor those of its characters, but through basic emotional responses.

'Ideas' are felt most profoundly as human concerns

It is, I think, in terms of these human feelings that we may see the 'ideas' approach working most successfully. It is when we see problems in human terms, affecting helpless creatures, that we feel the pathos of the human plight. This is the junction at which 'ideas' become a part of the larger sense of tragedy. The junction is particularly apparent with regard to the one important idea that I have not so far mentioned, Hardy's sense of man's decline. This belief in a general decline, a running-down of life, was widespread when Hardy was writing his later novels, and he is sometimes quite explicit in his endorsement of the belief. In *Tess* he found a localised expression for it in the decline of the d'Urberville family. This does not merely mean a social decline from being powerful landowners, but a decline of energy of some kind – of moral and spiritual strength. But we the readers feel this in personal, human terms. Tess's parents are feckless, drunken, ill-organised and ignorant. The girl herself has personal qualities which could raise her from this depth to which the family has declined. Instead she is sacrificed to the last throw of the dice on behalf of her d'Urberville past. In this way the idea of decline is woven intimately with that sense of tragic inevitability by which the book ultimately stands or falls as a work of art.

The pathos in the relationship between human beings and ideas is felt also in regard to those problems I discussed earlier. We may smile at the irony Hardy projects onto the religious convictions of many of his contemporaries, or regard them as cheap jibes, but the way in which these convictions are seen to affect Tess touches us much more deeply. Who can be unmoved by the makeshift baptism of her baby:

> She duly went on with the Lord's Prayer, the children lisping it after her in a thin gnat-like wail, till, at the conclusion, raising their voices to clerk's pitch, they again piped into the silence, 'Amen!'
>   Then their sister, with much augmented confidence in the efficacy of this sacrament, poured forth from the bottom of her heart the thanksgiving that follows, uttering it boldly and triumphantly in the stopt-diapason note which her voice acquired when her voice was in her speech, and which will never be forgotten by those who knew her. The ecstasy of faith almost apotheosized her . . .   [p.145]

Or who can fail to sympathise with her outrage at the parson's initial refusal to recognise the efficacy of a ceremony in which there is so much 'simple faith'? How much more powerful does the *idea* of loss of faith become when it is couched in these human terms:

> 'This reminds me, dear', she said. 'You remember you never would interfere with any belief of mine before we were married? But I knew your mind all the same, and I thought as you thought – not from any reasons of my own, but because you thought so. Tell me now, Angel, do you think we shall meet again after we are dead? I want to know.'
>   He kissed her to avoid a reply at such a time.
>   'O, Angel – I fear that means no!' said she, with a suppressed sob. 'And I wanted to see you again – so much, so much! What – not even you and I, Angel, who love each other so well?'   [pp.485–6]

Her last question sums up all the sorrow contained in the knowledge that strength of human feeling is no guarantee of immortality. The poignancy of the moment is given its background as an 'idea' immediately afterwards in Clare's response: 'Like a greater than himself, to the critical question at the critical time he did not answer . . .' [p.486] – for the man greater than himself is Christ, who died to give eternal life to all mankind who believe in him. But Christ was silent then as Clare is now, the modern unbeliever and the Saviour of 2000 years before brought together in their common moment of uncommitment.

Again, I do not think our feelings about Clare's predicament as a victim of the 'ache of modernism' are finally hostile to him. Even through his priggishness one must pity him, faced with a choice between views of life which were not of his making and unable to find any reconciliation. Three weeks after his marriage we find him brought face to face with a real human problem to which the great men of the past can give him no answer:

> After mechanically attempting to pursue his agricultural plans as though nothing unusual had happened, in the manner recommended by the great and wise men of all ages, he concluded that very few of those great and wise men had ever gone so far outside themselves as to test the feasibility of their counsel. 'This is the chief thing: be not perturbed', said that Pagan moralist. That was just Clare's own opinion. But he was perturbed. 'Let not your heart be troubled, neither let it be afraid', said the Nazarene. Clare chimed in cordially; but his heart was troubled all the same.   [p.332]

It is perhaps, then, the inadequacy of 'ideas' that gives them their greatest power in *Tess*. The tragic gap between what man sees and believes as an ideal for himself and the pathetic reality of his achievement seems to be a truth for all ages, not merely the nineteenth century, and its revelation makes for some of the most poignant moments in the novel.

'Formal' or 'Structural' approaches

When we discuss a novel in terms of its ideas, or its presentation of social themes, or (in certain aspects at least) in terms of the people in it, we are talking about the book's content, loosely speaking. A 'formal' or 'structural' approach decides to look primarily at the *way* the content is presented, rather than at the content for its own sake. 'Form' may manifest itself in a variety of ways: from quite technical matters such as the way the book is divided into chapters, through the choice of points of beginning and ending, the selection of a point of view, to the elusive and complicated matter of the very language of the novel itself.

'Form' versus 'content'

As soon as we begin to think about the matter, of course, a very tricky problem seems to present itself. When can we be sure we are talking about 'form' and not 'content'? We might well ask, indeed, whether it is possible to separate the two. To take language, for example: it would appear to be strange to talk about words as though they are only coverings for ideas or things, and as if by using a different word we leave the 'content' intact. For, surely, to use a different word is to produce, if ever so slightly, a different effect, and in consequence to mean something different. In which case form and content together would seem to make up 'meaning'; or, alternatively and more extremely, perhaps form *is* content – the way we say the thing is the meaning of the thing. This would be an extreme formalist position, and would imply that the *only* meaning to be found in a work of art (or at least the only *aesthetic* meaning) can be discovered in the form of that work. While at first glance such a position may seem unlikely to be tenable, it is in fact a very difficult attitude to argue against, and we must return to it later. For the present I shall assume that the formal approach is not the only critical stance, and that what we are dealing with is a point of view which looks *primarily* at structure, but may see it as complementary to other interpretations.

Henry James and point of view

Any critic who is considering the question of 'form' in the novel, particularly in the last quarter of the nineteenth century, will probably turn first to Hardy's great American contemporary, Henry James. James was the first modern novelist writing in English to take the problem of 'form' seriously, and indeed to take his special role as *artist* seriously. To say this is not to deny the seriousness of purpose of other nineteenth-century novelists. Clearly Dickens, Thackeray, Charlotte Brontë and George Eliot all believed that the things they were saying were important. But the difference from James is perhaps in that very belief. They saw themselves as writers with something to say: 'messages' which were contained in their novels and might teach or uplift their readers. Henry James saw the novelist as being first and foremost an artist, not a sage. As an artist he should be concerned primarily with the form of his work, the reason being that, according to James, it is only by selecting the right form that the content will be properly disclosed. This is not an easy idea to grasp, but an illustration which might help could be taken from one of James's favourite formal devices – 'point of view'. Henry James would claim that the point of view from which any story is told is crucial to its meaning. In the case of *Tess of the d'Urbervilles* Hardy has chosen a popular viewpoint, the more or less omniscient narrator. This allows him to be a flexible storyteller, moving about with his characters wherever they go, listening in on their conversations, seeing something of their thoughts and occasionally standing back to reflect on the action, on life in general, or on some abstract philosophical truth. If any single point of view is espoused rather than another, it is probably that of Tess, since Hardy is most sympathetic to her. But let us imagine that Hardy had told his story strictly through Tess's eyes – in the first person. This would give a very different complexion to the tale. First, on strictly practical grounds, we should know less about certain things. We could not accompany Angel Clare to his home and understand his background, see his parents – simply because Tess herself never went there. Correspondingly, of course, we should know a great deal more about Tess's feelings. We might understand more clearly what she felt about the two men in her life. The book would end, of course, not with Clare and Liza-Lu climbing the hill from Wintoncester, but in the condemned cell. It would perhaps be a gloomier story, and it would, even more than it is at present, be Tess's story. Or, to take a less likely case, suppose that Hardy had chosen Angel Clare as his storyteller. This would be truly to change the tale. We should now not know of Tess's affair with Alec or her baby until she revealed it to Clare – certainly a great moment of revelation, but hardly conveying the same kind of power as the scene written by Hardy.

My point is that, when we talk about telling the story from

different viewpoints, it can be argued that we are talking not about the same story but about a new story for each new point of view. Put simply, the story told by Clare would be Clare's story, not Tess's any longer. Henry James could therefore claim that there is not form and content, teller and thing told, but a single thing which is created by the selection of a point of view. The way it is told *is* the story. Point of view is only one aspect of form, though crucial for James. Its assumptions indicate James's general attitude to the work of art and the artist. For him, the novel should be a single whole – characters, action and narration all contributing to the total meaning of the work. Form is order, which gives definition to a work of art and presents it as something different from life. To quote James's own words (1920) 'Form alone *takes,* and holds and preserves, substance – saves it from the welter of helpless verbiage that we swim in as in a sea of tasteless tepid pudding, and that makes one ashamed of an art capable of such degradation'. (p.246). The best form is that which presents the meaning of the work of art most economically, which focuses our attention sharply upon the centre of interest, and does not let any of that interest ebb away in a 'leak': 'There is nothing so deplorable as a work of art with a *leak* . . .' (ibid).

I have spent some time in explaining James's ideas about form because, while they were the best-known exposition of the subject in 1891, they clearly do not apply very easily to the novels of Thomas Hardy. We have already encountered James's patronising attitude to Hardy, and one may understand why he felt superior. Hardy wrote as a popular novelist, unconstrained by James's high estimation of the artist. Far from highlighting the crucial centre of interest, he dissipates his energies in a plethora of subjects whose variety has been indicated in the first three sections of this book. In James's terminology, Hardy's novel 'leaks' in all directions. Are we to be interested in character, social history, ideas, sex and marriage, Christianity in the late nineteenth century? 'In all these things', Hardy would probably say, but for James such a claim is simply to relegate art to the messy, meaningless life from which it sprang.

Hardy's form may differ from James's

Are we to assume, then, that Hardy's novels have no form, or, at least, that to approach them in this way is not appropriate? I think we need not take up such a desperate position. All works of art have a form of some kind, and it is surely a mistake to condemn on Jamesian principles a novelist who is clearly not at all Jamesian in his art. Ian Gregor, in his book *The Great Web* (1974), has suggested that Hardy's novels have a form of their own which is quite different from the static, economy-oriented ideals of James. Gregor bases his view of Hardy on the idea of the story which is gradually unfolded before the reader. With this view go concepts of movement, becoming and process, rather than the Jamesian complete, homogenous work of art which can be 'walked round'. We walk *through* a Hardy novel, learning and changing as we go. 'Whereas in a James novel', says Gregor, 'we feel the work has already found its finest reader in the author, in Hardy the reading is still in process, the narrator's reading being only as sharp and as fitful as our own' (p.32). Gregor finds support for his view of the Hardy form in the author's own description of his novels as a 'series of seemings'. The phrase implies 'a seeking for a truth whose form is always provisional' (p.33). As a central condition of this kind of novel there is a relationship between the author and the reader, each acting upon the other in the process of discovery. It is significant that James's images for the novel's form are often taken from the plastic arts, which are fixed and unmoving. Hardy's key word, says Gregor, as against James's 'structure', is 'story'.

Gregor's interpretation of *Tess* emphasises, as we might expect, movement, change and instability. In the opening section of the novel, for example, he points to the fragmented nature of this pre-Fall life. It is not simply an Eden, but a world divided. It is a primitive world, but one within a four hours' journey from London. The girls who go club dancing are watched by young men who read *A Counterblast to Agnosticism*, while at home the reading is *The Compleat Fortune Teller*. Tess herself shows the duality of her nature when the family's horse is killed. She is like them in the dreamy state which leads to the accident, but unlike them in her self-accusation afterwards. More centrally, her relationship with Alec d'Urberville is ambiguous. She senses in Alec, says Gregor, 'her creator and her destroyer'. The question of whether she is raped or seduced must necessarily remain an open one, in order to preserve this ambiguity. But the sense of movement, rhythm is felt throughout the course of the book. Gregor believes that Hardy's words in *Tess* 'So do flux and reflux – the rhythm of change – alternate and persist in everything under the sky' [p.434] 'could well stand as an epigraph for both the manner and the matter of this novel' (p.198). Out of the consciousness of her past comes the special poignancy of Tess's wooing by Angel at Talbothays. This section deals with passion, but it would be wrong, says Gregor, to see it either simply as lyrical intensity or as a 'sardonic comment on the blindness of love' (p.185). Hardy holds a position somewhere between these two, which results in a feeling of 'the pure moment, cut off from the past, from all memory' (pp.189–90), but of course it *is* the past, memory, which holds the balance in this feeling. From this world of illusion and dream the reader is plunged into a world the very reverse. Flintcomb-Ash is an experience of the earth – hard, unrewarding, obdurate – and it metaphorises the phase itself entitled 'The Woman Pays'. But Tess will not give in. She tries 'to tell, and in the telling seek to understand' (p.191). She therefore goes to seek out Angel's parents, an abortive errand, and writes to her husband. In the final phase Gregor believes that *Tess* has found what its title indicates – 'fulfilment'. In one sense this is the fulfilment of 'nature's plan', but 'from another point of view it is Tess's own acceptance of herself . . . she has fused for Angel the image he adored with the woman he rejected' (p.196). The last image of the novel, with the two figures bowing to the earth and then continuing their journey hand in hand is for Gregor a vision of strength and resolution, an acceptance of the rhythms of 'nature' and a taking-up of the rhythms of human hope and fortitude – to go on. More than anything else, Gregor believes, the journey is a symbol of the form which he sees in the book – dependent on movement, change, rhythm, the encountering of new experiences and the juxtaposition of past and present.

I have perhaps done less than justice to the full subtlety of Gregor's argument, but there are two reasons for the comparative brevity of my description of his treatment of *Tess*, apart from obvious considerations of space. First, he raises a number of issues which are central to any general consideration of the novel, and I shall be touching on these issues in the second half of this book. Secondly, I wanted to give a strong sense of what seemed to me the main tendency of his argument on form as a contrast with Tony Tanner's approach, in his essay 'Colour and Movement in *Tess of the d'Urbervilles'* (1968).

But Hardy does also have Jamesian form

Tanner, in suggesting that a rather more Jamesian idea of 'form' *may* be applicable to *Tess,* begins his study by emphasising the 'incomparable clarity of Hardy's eyes' (p.183). Like Gregor, he cites Hardy's own claim to give shape to a 'series of seemings'; but, where Gregor emphasises the 'series', the sense of movement, Tanner feels that the 'seemings', the impressions made upon the eye, are the main formal features of Hardy's fiction. Explanations and ideas are secondary to what the eye tells us. Hardy achieves a kind of impersonality which Tanner believes is even greater than James's – the anonymity of folk tales or ballads – by presenting us not so much with a story of cause-and-effect as with a series of vivid scenes. In his words 'the overall architecture of the novel is blocked out with massive simplicity in a series of balancing phases – The Maiden, Maiden No More; The Rally, The Consequence; and so on'. (p.220). The expressions used here – 'architecture', 'blocked out', 'balancing' – are very reminiscent of a Jamesian approach to form. They emphasise plastic *shape* rather than movement, and the staticness of a gazer at something presented before him rather than a participator in changeable, unfolding events. Tanner compares Hardy's art to the words painted on walls and fences by a man in *Tess,* each word separated from the next by a comma. Just so are the series of 'prominent notations, and emphatic pauses which temporarily isolate, and thus vivify, key incidents and objects' in Hardy's novels.

Colour is of the first importance to an artist who works particularly from the visual, and Tanner takes as the first demonstration of his case Hardy's use of the colour red. In fact red is to be seen in conjunction with white, as we first witness it on Tess herself at the dance. She alone wears a red ribbon, which contrasts with the white of her dress and those of the other girls. She is therefore singled out to us from the first, and 'In that simple scene and colour contrast is the embryo of the whole book and all that happens in it' (p.221). In her youth Tess is frequently associated with whiteness. On the night of the rape she is a 'white muslin figure'. Her 'beautiful feminine tissue' is described as 'practically blank as snow'. The Vale in which the first events of the novel take place was known in former times as the Forest of the White Hart, an animal hunted to death like Tess herself. Red is identified specifically with blood at the moment when the Durbeyfields' horse is killed by the shaft of a cart which pierces his breast 'like a sword'. Tess, in trying to stanch the flow, is splashed herself with the crimson drops. We have seen that this moment in one sense is part of a cause-and-effect sequence. The family will now be almost destitute, and Tess is driven to 'seek kin' with the d'Urbervilles. But, says Tanner, the scene is far more powerful when read as an image. The piercing of Prince, with the subsequent flow of blood, looks forward to Tess's violation and the loss of blood she will suffer at the hands of Alec. After this release of the 'blood of innocence' Tess too will stand up like Prince 'as long as he could, till he suddenly sank down in a heap'.

It is obvious enough to say that red symbolises blood, in the sense of sexual passion, and white innocence and purity, but Tanner specifically rejects the symbolic overtones in favour of seeing such scenes as Prince's death as *omens*. Each omen is part of a cumulative pattern which builds up the sense of Tess's fate. So we have the red brick of the d'Urberville home looking forward to the red brick of the prison where she is hanged. Alec d'Urberville presses roses and strawberries upon her; a thorn on one of the roses pricks her chin. The words of ill omen are painted on walls and fences in red paint. The threshing-machine to which Tess is tied, metaphorically, is a 'buzzing red glutton'. She strikes Alec and draws blood, only to strike him at the end and mortally spill his heart's blood, which shows itself as a terrible ace of hearts on the ceiling below. There is nevertheless a symbolic element in the use of colour by Hardy, and Tanner recognises it. Stabbing may mean death or procreation – both let out blood. Tess's blood frequently rises as a blush, suggesting passion, but blood released is also death: 'Life starts in sex and ends in death, and Hardy constantly shows how closely allied the two forms of blood-letting are in one basic, unalterable rhythm of existence' (p.226).

Contrast between Tanner and Gregor

Both Gregor and Tanner see movement as central to the

structure of *Tess*, but to understand how they differ in their conception of this image is to understand something of the difference between their two ideas of form. Gregor sees movement as the journey, the encountering of experience. Tanner's vision is of the figure in the landscape – 'a moving spot on the white vacuity', as Hardy puts it. For him, we are not ourselves caught up in the movement, but stand looking at scenes in which movement is reduced to a picture, something seen. Tanner is in fact making even movement a part of Hardy's static, visual technique. So we see figures caught for an instant on the road – Tess's father as the book opens, Tess herself pausing with her heavy load (a static type-figure to be read as a picture, a little like Christian at the opening of *The Pilgrim's Progress*). The tendency of this emphasis on the static, visual quality is to make us see the larger, general movement behind the particular instant, so Tess *is* a figure, or even a 'moving spot', in a large, silent landscape. As an upright, moving thing she is that principle of life which is only eradicated when she (and we) lie down and become one with the horizontal lines of earth – in death. This movement is adumbrated in various moments throughout the book, culminating in her lying on the sacrificial altar at Stonehenge. Tess must wander because she has no home, until she finds her last home – the other side of the door to her ancestors' vaults, of which barrier she had once said, 'Why am I on the wrong side of this door!' [p.449].

The tendency of Tanner's interpretation is obviously strongly affective. The emphasis is not on the intricacies of causes, whether they be social or personal, but on our perception of the great truths of existence. Tess running after Angel, 'a moving spot on the white vacuity', is for Tanner 'a visible paradigm of the terms of human life', and we are to understand the novel primarily in the way we are affected by our perception of things as vast as life, procreation and death. To shift the burden of the book's meaning so thoroughly from the particular to the general, the causative to the affective, may make some readers unhappy, but we shall leave this problem, so central to *Tess*, for later and fuller discussion.

Language as form

Both Ian Gregor and Tony Tanner approach the idea of 'form'

in the novel with the assumption that it is to be found in *imitation*. That novels are a convincing imitation of life is perhaps the fact about them that most people would recognise before all else. So we might expect that the shape given to his work by a novelist would be some version of the shape of life, scenes and colours which imprint themselves upon the eye, or the unrolling of events. If we think about language as the basic form of a literary work, we are more likely to turn to the poem, in which the imitative element is not so apparent. Poems are less likely to be narrative, to contain realistic dialogue and fully developed characters; and, if they do contain these things, we are likely to have our attention distracted from them by lineation, metre, rhyme, or simply the unnatural 'density' of poetic language, which tends to be more elliptical and have a greater number of images than everyday language. The novelist is drawn two ways, as regards not only language but the whole of his art. On the one hand he must make his representation of life as convincingly 'ordinary' as possible; on the other, he is bound to select and shape in order to give meaning to that representation. How does this affect the kind of language he uses? In certain localised forms it is plain to see that there has been a conscious selecting of words by the novelist, and to that extent a manipulation of language. Taking, for example, proper names, we know that Hardy rejected a number of names for his heroine before deciding on the one which for some reason suited him best. The unusual name 'Angel Clare' (he plays a harp!) probably has ironic overtones. Expanding this to a larger theme, we might remark on the high incidence of curious names in Hardy's fiction, and relate it to his general preoccupation with the odd and grotesque. Proper nouns are not the only words which may be clearly symbolic. We have already seen that 'red' is used as a pattern in the book, but here we find ourselves at that crucial boundary between the 'thing' and the 'word for the thing'. Strictly speaking, when Hardy uses the word 'red' he is creating a pattern not of language but of colour, a property to which our senses respond. Probably the most we can claim for language here is that it is a necessary tool, as when Hardy describes Tess as 'untinctured' by experience, 'untinctured' drawing attention to a whole metaphoric pattern of colour which was in Hardy's mind as he wrote.

If we wish to claim that the language of a novel is truly

significant as the form of that novel, then we shall be involved in
an effort to relate the structure of the language in some detail to
the overall meaning of the book, and dealing with such things as
syntax, lexis and rhythm. We shall be hoping to give some sense
of the particular novelist's style – in fact, endeavouring to
establish what makes his use of language distinctive. A good
deal may be said about a novelist's style, and many novelists,
including Hardy, have very distinctive styles. But it is less likely
that a single novel will have a style peculiarly its own. When we
have established some features of a novelist's style, this may tell
us something about *him* as a writer, but not a lot about language
as the form of one particular novel. Exactly the same might be
said of a poet with regard to one of his poems, but with the
crucial difference that it is much easier to analyse the poem as
an individual language construct than to analyse the novel in
this way. A whole novel is simply too long to examine word by
word, or even phrase by phrase, and it is unlikely that it would
be a really rewarding exercise throughout. Faced with an
apparently colourless piece of dialogue between two fictional
characters, which is apparently merely intended to carry the
story forward, or illustrate some thematic point, it is hard to
believe that the words could not have been arranged differently
without losing any of the point.

A selective approach

These problems have not deterred David Lodge, who in his
book *Language of Fiction* (1966) claims that

> if we are right to regard the art of poetry as essentially an art
> of language, then so is the art of the novel; and . . . the critic of
> the novel has no special dispensation from that close and
> sensitive engagement with language which we naturally
> expect from the critic of poetry . . .   (p.47)

In reply to the suggestion that a novel cannot be held totally in
the mind of the reader, he would say that neither is a poem
susceptible of such a feat. Both must be subjected to a *selective*
consideration of their language, though probably the critic
must be more drastically selective with a novel. Lodge's
solution to the problem of dealing with a large prose work in

terms of its language is to try to see patterns running through the whole work, but to illustrate this overview with close analysis of certain passages. He also identifies a certain principle – 'repetition' – as being crucial to linguistic analysis in the novel. Clearly it is not possible to do more here than indicate Lodge's methods through the use he makes of them when discussing *Tess*, since they involve detailed discussion of certain passages. Broadly speaking, he attempts to demonstrate that Hardy's most notorious 'faults' – his reliance on contrived situation, his authorial intrusions, his reliance on stock characters – are all involved in a basic failure of language: poor writing, in fact. The heart of this 'poor writing' is a duality in Hardy. As narrator he can create on the one hand flawlessly authentic dialect, and on the other he can be a clumsily self-conscious 'stylist' with laboured syntax and pedantic vocabulary. This second 'voice' is not always a bad thing, but, claims Lodge, as the medium for a number of generalised points of view – 'sceptical philosopher, and local historian, topographer, antiquarian' (p.169) – it often clashes with the 'voice of the author as creator and maker, one acquainted with the deepest interior processes of his characters' minds' (p.170). This unease is manifested in Hardy's hesitation about how far he should try to adopt the tone Tess herself might have used when he is rendering her thoughts. A passage such as this is hardly a simple country girl's language: 'It just crossed her mind, too, that he might have a faint recollection of his tender vagary, and was disinclined to allude to it from a conviction that she would take amatory advantage of the opportunity it gave her of appealing to him anew not to go'. [p.322]. On occasion Hardy feels it necessary to interpolate a kind of apology–explanation for the unlikeliness of Tess's thoughts:

> She thought, *without exactly wording the thought,* how strange and godlike was a composer's power, who from the grave could lead through sequences of emotion, which he alone had felt at first, a girl like her who had never heard of his name, and never would have a clue to his personality.   (p.134; emphasis added)

By means of some detailed analysis, Lodge suggests that

Hardy's confusion about the meaning of 'Nature' in the novel is reflected linguistically also, particularly in a confusion in the handling of point of view. The images which associate Tess with Nature clash with the detached 'guide-book' tone which Hardy often adopts when speaking of landscape. Hardy ultimately, says Lodge, 'undermines our trust in the reliability of Tess's response to Nature, which is his own chief rhetorical device for defending her character and interesting our sympathies on her behalf' (p.178).

Is Hardy's language a strength or a weakness?

It is unfortunate, perhaps, that, in the case of Hardy, Lodge's attempt to demonstrate the essentially linguistic nature of the novelist's art should result in such a negative response. For the 'confusion' which Lodge sees in Hardy in general – the clumsy plotting and so on – may be (and has been) seen by many critics as a vitality in the writer which marks his special sense of the oddity of life. Such an interpretation is not necessarily undermined by Lodge's demonstration that it is a 'confusion' at language level. Ian Gregor has taken issue with Lodge's interpretation of a much-discussed passage, in which Tess is seen wandering about in the early morning at Talbothays. Where Lodge sees confusion, Gregor finds a rich complexity, by avoiding a paragraph-by-paragraph analysis in favour of a 'reading through' of several paragraphs: 'It is the difference between seeing "stills" from a film and seeing that film in motion' (p.187).

There are surely two points here which rather work against Lodge's claims for the primacy of language as 'form' in the novel. First, similar interpretations of a passage may result in totally different conclusions (Gregor agrees with the details of Lodge's analysis). Secondly, linguistic analysis seems prone to be used, consciously or unconsciously, as a tool to back up assumptions the writer already entertains about the novel, rather than as an autonomous means of discovery. Finally, I would contend (and I think Lodge would agree) that he is talking about 'style', and, as I have suggested, this may not amount to more than a general indication of the commoner linguistic features of a writer, whenever and whatever he is writing, not a revelation of the form of a specific novel.

A 'genetic' approach

Strengths and weaknesses

The following section presents a very different approach to the novel from those which have gone before. Broadly speaking, the basis of the stance taken by these previous critics has been 'impressionistic'. They work from the impression given them by a reading of the text. When they consider the whole work, certain themes, ideas, actions or people are found particularly striking, and upon these impressions their picture of the novel's 'meaning' is built. The kind of criticism we are now about to consider does not begin with the simple assumption of a single text. The 'genetic' approach, as its name implies, is concerned with the way the novel evolved through the various stages from manuscript to printed versions. There is therefore a basis of verifiable fact denied, at least to the same extent, to the 'impressionistic' critic. It would be hoped that with the 'genetic' approach we might be able to deduce from the history of Hardy's composition of his novel certain facts upon which critical opinions could be based. In so far as we *are* dealing with intransigent fact, the critical results are, I think, bound to be more tentative than the 'impressionist' would claim for his methods. There is, for instance, no arguing with the presence of a certain change of wording in a manuscript, but the very certainty of this fact limits what may be derived from it critically. The 'genetic' approach is perhaps to be seen rather as a critical tool than as an interpretation in itself. If this is felt to be a limitation, it should be remembered that the 'genetic' critic is perhaps forced by his approach to be more pragmatic than the 'impressionist'. Instead of beginning with an idea, and fitting the text around it, he takes the stages in the writing and printing of the text and sees what may and may not be deduced from the evidence.

We are fortunate, in the case of *Tess of the d'Urbervilles*, in having a very thorough example of 'genetic' criticism. This is J. T. Laird's *The Shaping of Tess of the d'Urbervilles* (1975), which examines in considerable detail not only the manuscript stages of the novel's composition, but also the history of its publication in a number of editions up to the 'Wessex' of 1912. Laird himself gives three advantages which his method has over more traditional approaches. First, we may understand the meaning of the definitive text better by studying the author's creative processes. Secondly, we may understand more fully the reasons for the unevenness in Hardy's writing, and the causes of both the strengths and the weaknesses. Finally, Laird's approach reveals the gap between Hardy the novelist who wanted to be honest and clear in his work and the Hardy who seemed to try to mislead the public about the composition of his work – especially in his official 'biography' (really mainly an autobiography under his second wife's name). As readers concerned with a literary critical assessment of the novel, our interest will, I think, mainly be centred on the first two of these, and perhaps especially the first.

Hardy's effects not always intentional

There is, of course, no space here to enter into all Laird's analyses of the layers of manuscripts and states of the text in various editions, but it is possible, by some selection of examples, to demonstrate what *kind* of critical judgements may be made using 'genetic' methods. First, there is at least one general point which may be demonstrated from the textual history of *Tess*, which is that the effects the novelist produces are not always a direct result of any artistic intentions. When Hardy decided that he was going to have to compromise with the moral standards of the editor of a 'family magazine' if he was to attain the financial rewards of publication in one of them, he set about bowdlerising his text extensively, with a view to gaining the approval of the editor of the *Graphic*. It was in the *Graphic*, indeed, that the novel first appeared. Even while the novel was first appearing as a serial, however, its author was busy restoring the text to its original form for the first edition (that is, as a book). But, as Laird points out, Hardy was less than honest in the account he gave of the business, suggesting that he simply restored the original pre-*Graphic* readings throughout. What he neglected to mention is that many of the changes he made when adapting the manuscript for the *Graphic* were *permanent* alterations. The most significant point about this is that some of the artistic flaws in the book version of the novel are a result of elements Hardy introduced with the more lurid tastes of the serial reader in mind, and which were carried over into the first and subsequent editions. For, while family magazines such as the *Graphic* forbade the inclusion of sexual material, sensationalism and even violence were not taboo. Such incidents might include Angel's crossing the flooded river Frome in his sleep, the appearance of Alec as an evangelical preacher, and the bloodstain on the ceiling after his murder.

The growth of Tess as a character

More central to our concern, however, are those gradual shapings of the novel which show something of Hardy's developing concerns and intentions. These are most marked in the matter of character, and in particular the nature of his heroine. Broadly, there seems to have been a gradual 'refining, ennobling and idealising' of Tess's character on Hardy's part throughout the history of his composition of the novel. Initially he may have been concerned with bowderlising his text for the *Graphic,* but this is subordinate to his increasing interest in the portrayal of his heroine. For example, he emphasises her courage, both physical and moral. The former is suggested by amendments such as '"Safe thank God in spite of your folly!" said she, her face on fire', for simply 'Safe thank God' (Laird, p.126), when Alec drives her recklessly down the hill. Her moral courage is suggested in the phrases used to describe her unbuttoning her dress to suckle her baby. Originally these were, 'with a curious, stealthy movement, and rising of colour', but they were later amended to 'with a curious, stealthy, yet courageous movement, and rising of colour' (ibid.). A further dignity is given to Tess by the new emphasis, in later stages of the manuscript, on her d'Urberville ancestry, and her modesty also becomes more apparent. When Clare clasps her unexpectedly in his arms, Hardy first wrote, 'she panted in her impressionability and burst into a succession of ecstatic sobs', but later amended this to 'she sank upon him in her momentary joy, with something very like an ecstatic cry' (Laird, p.128).

Hardy's own commitment to Tess, both moral and personal, also grew as the story developed from the earliest manuscripts. His first attitude appears to have been 'for the most part one of moral neutrality' (Laird, p.122), but, as we have seen, he added, just before the first edition, his famous subtitle and epigraph. One of the most fascinating examples of his increasing the note of personal involvement with Tess is his inclusion of the phrase 'and which will never be forgotten by those who knew her' when describing Tess's voice at the baptism of her child. It is completely absent from the manuscripts and entered the text of the first edition via his writing up of the baptism scene for separate publication, since he had been forced to excise the scene for serial publication in the *Graphic*.

The history of Hardy's modifications of Tess's character did not end with the first edition, for he seems to have been spurred on to the defence of his 'pure' heroine by the attacks of some early reviewers, notably that by Mowbray Morris in the *Quarterly Review*. In his diary Hardy remarked, 'Well, if this sort of thing continues no more novel-writing for me. A man must be a fool to deliberately stand up to be shot at' (Laird, p.174); but in practical terms he fought back, with the Preface to the fifth edition, dated July 1892. The general complaint of Morris had been concerned with the supposed coarseness of the novel, and had centred particularly on the notorious single word 'pure': 'It is indisputably open to Mr Hardy to call his heroine a pure woman; but he has no less certainly offered many inducements to his readers to refuse her the name' (ibid).

Hardy replied vigorously in his Preface, emphasising 'the acts of a woman in her last days of desperation, when all her doings lie outside her normal character' (Laird, p.175), and the challenge was supported by the changes he made to the text when it appeared in September 1892. Not only is the whole treatment of the sexual themes in the book more explicit, but the tendency is to make Tess more clearly a victim of others' violence. The italicised words in the following passage were now included for the first time: '*He knelt and bent lower, till her breath warmed his face, and in a moment his cheek was in contact with hers*. She was sleeping soundly, *and upon her eyelashes there lingered tears*' (Laird, p.176). This suggestion of force is made even more explicitly a matter of rape by the inclusion of the comment of one of the women workers as she watches Tess with her baby in the fields: 'A little more than persuading had to do wi' the coming o't, I reckon. There were they that heard a sobbing one night last year in The Chase; and it mid ha' gone hard wi' a certain party if folks had come along' [p.140].

Obviously such modifications increase our sympathy for Tess, and make the epithet 'pure' more acceptable in all but the most narrowly physical sense of the word. Hardy continued the 'refinement' of his heroine even up to the edition of 1912, where most of her speech outside her own home becomes free of dialect. This was a direct result of a modification in the fifth edition, where for the first time the reader was told she 'spoke two languages; the dialect at home, more or less; ordinary English abroad and to persons of quality' [p.185].

Problems with Angel's character

If the successive manuscript-layers and editions of the novel served to increase Hardy's commitment to his heroine, they seemed to provide only greater problems with her husband's character. Some of the inconsistencies in Clare's character were intended as a demonstration of his humanness, and are simply part of a complex personality at a problematic time of life in difficult circumstances. But some of Hardy's changes to his manuscript show him to have been uncertain about Clare's character – in particular about the kind and degree of his love for Tess. When, for example, Tess is musing on Angel's restraint, we see the manuscript going through various alterations as Hardy attempts to establish *for himself* just what is motivating the young man. Tess (or Rose-Mary as she is in the earlier manuscript-layers) feels a 'tender respect' for

> *perhaps*
> the purity of mind
> *& chivalrous sense of duty shown by Angel Clare, qualities*
> & slight coldness of nature which she had never expected to find in one of the opposite sex   (Laird, p.134)

In this, 'perhaps' was introduced, only to be cancelled, together with the whole suggestion of a 'slight coldness of nature', for which the 'chivalrous sense of duty' was substituted. But in the first edition both the 'purity of mind' and the 'chivalrous sense of duty' disappeared, to be replaced by 'what she deemed the self-controlling sense of duty'. And finally this was again modified by the phrase 'rightly or wrongly' in the fifth edition, so that the final reading is 'what she deemed, rightly or wrongly, the self-controlling sense of duty . . .'. This is a single example, but it indicates that Hardy has doubts about what kind of young man Clare was. Perhaps to some extent his increasing commitment to a pure and victimised Tess made it increasingly difficult to justify Angel Clare's treatment of her.

Does he lack passion? Hardy's descriptions of him frequently deny this. But the author uneasily toys with some kind of modification of his sexual commitment. 'Spiritual', 'purity', 'coldness of nature', 'fastidious' are all words which occur at various times to suggest some explanation of his conduct, but finally there must remain an inconsistency, or perhaps it would be more accurate to say an uncertainty, about just what makes Clare the person he is. This point has a particular relevance, as we shall see, because it suggests a problem with 'causality' which is perhaps central to this novel. Tess as victim need only display the passive features of persecuted innocence (though she is more than this). But those who bring on her misfortunes must be active, and understood as people with motivation and commitment. Hardy also found problems in deciding what kind of a person Alec d'Urberville was, and it would seem that in both cases the difficult was one of causality.

Modification of authorial comment

A fact which may be somewhat surprising is revealed by comparison of the various versions of the text. Hardy had included from the first a good deal of authorial commentary, some of it fairly unobtrusive, but a fairly large proportion of a general philosophical kind, in which he speaks as a committed commentator. A passage such as that asking 'where was Tess's guardian angel?' is typical, and has been cited already. Many commentators have remarked disparagingly on such commentary, and it would seem that it increased in bitterness through the various manuscript-layers and early editions, in response to the popular prejudices of his age as encountered by Hardy in some of the first reviews. In fact, however, Hardy seems in the first edition to have attempted some modification of his authorial intrusions. He excluded this, for example: 'Their [Angel's brothers] presence here at Marlott at this hour, though it had no bearing upon the nearer events which followed, was regarded as singular in later years, when viewed by the light of certain incidents' (Laird, p.172). And the manuscript comment 'an attractive phase in all her sex', a qualification of 'standing, moreover, on the momentary threshold of womanhood', is also omitted. 'The material distinctions of rank and wealth he commendably despised' becomes '. . . increasingly despised'; 'she' is substituted for 'the poor girl'. These and other examples seem to point to a Hardy who was aware of a need for greater objectivity, and as a corollary perhaps also suggests that those comments he left in were sufficiently important for him not to touch them, or even, as we have seen, to increase their potency.

'Genetic' criticism is pragmatic and concerned with intentions.

These, then, are some of the particular results which may be achieved from a 'genetic' approach. But what are the more general characteristics of genetic criticism, particularly when compared with more traditional 'impressionistic' methods? Clearly the process of reading a novel in a number of versions, some of them manuscript, and carefully comparing key passages, is one which calls for time, patience and painstaking attention to detail. And when this is completed the results may be somewhat meagre compared to a full-scale 'interpretation' of the novel. For, as I suggested earlier, perhaps the most striking difference between the first four sections and the present one is that we are unlikely to achieve any startling new readings of the work from 'genetic' criticism. It begins with the 'states', or stages of composition, of the text, and makes pragmatic observations on it. A further important characteristic of this kind of criticism is that its emphasis is necessarily on the *intentions* of the novelist. I say 'necessarily' because in examining changes in the text made by the author himself we must always be involved in some way with intention. The intention to change may of course be forced on the writer, as was the case with the bowderlisations for the *Graphic,* but even these may tell us something – for example, that some of these changes were retained in later versions, and were therefore for some reason part of the author's later intention.

What may we deduce about Hardy's *artistic* intentions in *Tess?* If we take the figure of Tess herself, we are certainly aware of his close commitment to her, and sense of her as a real person, increasing if anything as he continued adding and revising. We see him also emphasising her position as victim, her purity and her sensitivity, driven as he was to a more firm statement of these things in the face of hostile criticism.

The value of establishing the author's intention

It may be asked, of course, how this can help the reader

critically. Does the author's intention matter, since one might say the book becomes 'public property' on publication, and it is up to each reader to make up his own mind about it? And that reader might well hold that he is perfectly aware from the cumulative evidence of the single definitive text, that Tess is a victim and is sensitive and 'pure', and that he does not need to be told that Hardy *intended* this effect. In fact almost all the authorial changes are going to reinforce the impression made by the definitive text, so any contemplation of such changes is bound to reinforce that impression. Given this, however, the evidence of the text has an indisputable force. If, for example, a reader wished to deny that Tess was presented as 'pure', or as a victim, he would have to argue against the manifest intentions of the author. Laird's conclusions may not be revolutionary, but they are hard to dispute, and they lay down a groundwork for viewing the evolution of the book upon which more adventurous, impressionistic theories may take their stand.

This 'instrumental' function of genetic criticism, its value as an aid in conjunction with other approaches, is seen also in its ability to show up artistic problems. We can understand from Laird's evidence that Hardy was clearly uncertain about Angel Clare as a character. This does not of course prevent D. H. Lawrence from forming an elaborate 'mythos' about the young man and his relations with Tess, nor prevent De Laura from seeing him as a representative of a late Arnoldian 'ache of modernism'. But in one way or another that authorial uncertainty must affect our judgement of these views, whether we see it as a vital irresolution (we never completely understand human beings in life, either) or adjudge it a considerable artistic flaw, leaving us unsatisifed with our lack of clear understanding.

The most subtle benefit of Laird's approach is perhaps one attributable not to specific changes, but rather to the overall sense of the work of art which is imparted to us. In tracing through the manuscripts and editions we feel the growth of the work of art as a living thing, and understand that it is not simply the final 'definitive' text on the page, but something which has evolved from hints, ideas, affections, a sense of weakness in various parts, and outside pressures.

Part Two
Appraisal

HOW can the reader, faced with so many different points of view on one work of fiction, begin to make any final value judgements? It would seem that for every weakness in a critical approach, encouraging the reader to discount it, a strength may be cited which forces him to give some credence to the argument. I believe that it is the glory of the appreciation of literature (and of all the arts) that there are no absolute rights and wrongs. We are not concerned with awarding and deducting points to be added up so that the victor's crown may be awarded by half a mark. There is something of value in every view of *Tess of the d'Urbervilles* which I have outlined, as also some limitation. Our aim must be to attempt some synthesis of the best which will not distort the separate points of view involved, nor be simply an imposed patchwork of ideas. Above all we must not forget that the only ultimate aim of the critic is to let the work of art itself live more fully for every reader.

Interdependence of approaches

Obviously the 'approaches' of the first section do not exclude one another absolutely. The argument that the novel is about the opposition between 'natural' and 'unnatural' may be supported by a 'formal' view which sees images as the basis of the novel. So the visual image of Tess on the threshing-machine is, looked at one way, a sociological 'message', but seen in another way is part of a structure of symbols for the subjugation of Tess. Again, the problems of an economic and historical kind which are seen as so central by Kettle and Williams ('social' approaches) are perhaps to some degree complementary with the approach which sees the history of ideas as a key to the characters' dilemma. And both these views must touch on the characters of Tess, Angel and Alec, who are the products of history and economics, and who hold ideas. That so many different interpretations should be viable without necessarily excluding one another is of course a sign of the novel's richness and complexity, but at the same time there are lines of distinction to be drawn which cannot easily be crossed. I see these dividing-lines as being of two kinds in *Tess*. The first defines the opposition between different views of what causes the tragedy, and the second distinguishes between a 'causal' view itself and an 'affective' interpretation.

Two leading impressions have remained throughout the critical history of *Tess of the d'Urbervilles*. The first is the powerful sense of tragedy evoked by the novel; the second is a certain sense of a final artistic failure. Perhaps 'failure' is too strong a word. The feeling is rather that suggested by David Lodge when he says that Hardy might be described as an 'in spite of' novelist. Very few critics seem able to put their full critical commitment behind Hardy as a complete artist. We have already heard Henry James speak of *Tess* as being 'chock-full of faults and falsity'. Other critics have found Hardy great 'in spite of' his linguistic clumsiness, his pedantic or pseudo-philosophical or glibly cynical authorial intrusions, his reliance upon unlikely coincidence and upon stock melodramatic characters. Yet the least sympathetic of these commentators finds it difficult to deny the tragic power of the novel. Kettle may be narrow in his interpretation, but the socio-economic destruction he sees clearly strikes him with a terrible sense of human loss. Raymond Williams records the same note of destruction, though his slant is different. And those critics who focus on individual human experience as the centre of the novel see that experience as movingly tragic. For Lawrence Tess is destroyed by two men, for Roy Morrell by her own moral inadequacies. Even so celebratory a view of the heroine as that of Irving Howe can only demonstrate the human potential represented by Tess. The tragedy is that this potential is wasted.

'Tragedy' implying causes

Tragedy, however, is a large word; it contains more than one meaning, and how we interpret the tragedy of *Tess of the d'Urbervilles* is, I think, crucial to understanding what seems to me the greatest bone of contention in this 'critics' debate'. To take only the instances I have mentioned in the last paragraph, we should seem to have a number of different versions of 'tragedy'. For Kettle and Williams, I presume, the tragic experience lies in witnessing some kind of inevitable process beyond the power of the individual to control. In the case of Kettle, at least, the victimisation of the heroine only stands as a focus for a greater victimisation, one which has affected all our lives, and perhaps still does so. For Roy Morrell the emphasis on inevitability is replaced by a feeling of failed responsibility. Our tragic awareness is that something *could* have been, but is painfully denied by the heroine's moral weakness at moments of choice. Lawrence restores the element of inevitability, but places it in the subconscious feelings of the protagonists. They are drawn towards each other fatally by something perhaps in part inherited, in part their deepest needs. We feel, as against Morrell's interpretation, that these needs are so much a part of them that they could not be the human beings they are without such destructive drives. What all these views share, however, (with the exception of Howe's), and have in common with De Laura's 'ache of modernism' account, is that they look at tragedy, or at least *this* tragedy, as a matter primarily of causes. For them, to investigate and explain how the thing came about is to convey the sense of the thing. Tragedy for them lies first and foremost in the action and the characters. These things are the repositories of tragedy, so that we can say Tess is a tragic figure, referring to something which is within her, *whatever our apprehension of her might be*.

'Tragedy' as an effect

But here is a very different version of tragedy. In this it is we, the witnesses, who make the action tragic, because our emotions have been tragically affected. This version of the tragic experience perhaps receives its clearest (and certainly its oldest) exposition in the writings of Aristotle. In his essay *On the Art of Poetry*, Aristotle writes of tragedy as 'by means of pity and fear bringing about the purgation of such emotions' (1965 translation, p.39). In fact he is far from ignoring the 'causative' aspects of tragedy, for he defines just what should arouse these emotions in the audience. The tragic hero should be a very specific kind of person: 'This is the sort of man who is not conspicuous for virtue and justice, and whose fall into misery is not due to vice and depravity, but rather to some error . . .' (p.48), but it is the stress he places on the 'affective' power of tragedy – the way its moves the audience – which is important in relation to *Tess*. While we cannot help being drawn to ask *why* Tess finds herself in such unfortunate situations, I believe it is more important for our appreciation of the novel that we should be powerfully aware of her *being* in the situation. It is our awareness which moves us to pity and fear, if we feel such emotions. In the pages which follow, I should like to put forward the case for an 'affective' reading of *Tess*. While this means that to some extent I must play down the importance of causes, I think it will be possible to show that the two approaches are not incompatible, in part because the affective may include the narrowly causative, and in part because the affective may draw our attention to causes of a larger and more transcendent kind.

The weaknesses of 'Tess' mainly causal

My first task is to suggest why I am inclined to give less credence to a causative reading of *Tess* than an affective. Broadly, it seems to me that it is precisely as a tragedy of causation that the novel's weaknesses are most apparent. For many people the most forced, least credible parts of Tess are those in which the author is showing *how* things came to be as they are for the heroine. This is particularly apparent in the matter of plot and action. There is often a complex interconnectedness between various people and events which seems scarcely credible. Alec d'Urberville, for example, reappears in Tess's life at a crucial moment. He has been converted to an extreme religiosity by Angel Clare's father. He pursues Tess to the farm on which she is working, and where her employer happens to be the very man whom Clare had knocked down some months before. Tess happens to see Angel's two brothers and Mercy Chant when she goes to seek help from her parents-in-law; they happen to talk about her, and happen to see her boots (and appropriate them). Now it is well known that novels often depend upon a higher degree of coincidence than we might feel was stricly natural, but it is difficult not to feel that Hardy has manipulated the action of *Tess* because he wants to suggest some pattern of doom for the heroine. Such a feeling is supported by Tess's spending her honeymoon in an abandoned seat of the d'Urbervilles, by seeing d'Urberville portraits whose removal is precluded by their being built into the wall, and most notoriously by the letter she writes to Clare, and which slips under the carpet. In so far as 'plotting' is the means by which the backbone of cause-and-effect is set up in a novel, a good deal of the plot in *Tess* would seem to be manufactured with too little thought for 'organic' causality – that is, without sufficient attention being paid to the natural unfolding of events. It must be said, however, that there is an appeal open to those who would support Hardy's manipulation of plot. It may be claimed that for Hardy 'the natural unfolding of events' is precisely as he demonstrates it to be. Coincidence may be a means of showing how man is dependent on chance rather than on providence, and in fact Hardy may be suggesting that life is essentially as grotesque as his somewhat twisted and inturned plot suggests. In other words, what is often seen as a weakness may be a formal device. Such an interpretation cannot be ignored, but I think it should be borne in mind that the emphasis is thereby thrown not onto a particular cause, but onto a far more general feeling that this is 'the nature of things' – a stance more in tune, I think, with an affective interpretation, as we shall see.

It is not only in crossing Tess's path, by fate or chance, that Alec d'Urberville may be seen as a weak link in the novel. We have already seen that a number of critics have found his melodramatic character hard to accept. It could well seem that Hardy, faced with the need to have his heroine seduced in order to precipitate the series of causes and effects which result in her eventual death, invented a convenient stock figure who would seduce, pursue, bribe and eventually be stabbed by Tess. We have seen from Lawrence's criticism that this is not all that may be said about Alec, but he does again seem in himself to associate causality with the weaker aspects of Hardy's art. Curiously, a defence may be found in that episode which seems least credible in a somewhat incredible character – his conversion to, and perversion from, Christianity. It might be argued that, as with the plot, the very grotesqueness of these events is part of a 'world view' which sees life itself as grotesque. We certainly know from other novels that Hardy was interested in extreme and unstable characters. On balance, however, the convenience of the business may well be felt to outweigh its thematic significance. I think that really we are interested in Alec primarily as an 'instrument', not for his own sake.

Perhaps the least satisfactory aspect of Alec, causally speaking, is his death. This is a good illustration of how Hardy seems concerned with the effect of an event rather than the cause. It is important for him that Tess should finally die, and die a victim of the society which has disowned and persecuted her. The poignantly short interlude in which she and Angel live in the unoccupied house during their flight, the dramatic bloodstain on the ceiling, the last night spent at Stonehenge, and the final moment of Clare and Liza-Lu walking up the hill from the jail together, are all impossible without the murder of Alec. And yet why should Tess commit such an act? Ultimately, it would seem, as a result of Angel's visit: 'He heard me crying about you, and he bitterly taunted me; and called you by a foul name; and then I did it' [pp.474–5].

But here we perhaps find ourselves in deeper water. Can Angel be such a wonderful human being that a woman would kill for him in a fit of despair at having lost his love? 'To her he was, as of old, all that was perfection, personally and mentally' [p.475]. Angel seems woefully short of this ideal, and somehow it must lessen Tess's tragic stature to accept such a man so uncritically. In this case, I think, what is affectively necessary is causally suspect.

Hardy's own confusion about causes

More than anything else, we are perhaps inclined to look askance at causal interpretations of the novel because of the very multiplicity of causes, which amounts at times to a positive confusion. Is Tess a victim of society? Certainly Hardy's own comments would seem at times to bear out such a view: 'She had been made to break an accepted social law, but no law known to the environment in which she fancied herself such an anomaly' [p.135]. But equally he sometimes seems to suggest that the cyclical nature of history is to blame. The once-proud d'Urbervilles are now despoiled themselves. Or are we to take the innumerable omens in the book, from Angel's missed dance with Tess to an afternoon cock-crow, as an indication that some mysterious fate pursues mankind (or is it the heroine only)? Character perhaps is responsible for events, but whose character, and what aspect of it? Is it an act of tragic nobility on Tess's part to tell Angel her past, or is she morally reprehensible for not telling him sooner? Is Tess merely a victim of the defective characters of other people? Or is the ultimate cause to be traced to specific historical and economic conditions in the nineteenth century? It is not impossible to suggest, of course, that all these things play their part in the tragedy. But they are not always strictly compatible. If we are the victims of Fate, we cannot be responsible for our own actions, and the impact of localised economic forces is considerably lessened if we have to believe also that history is simply cyclical, with the irony that may imply. There are problems of focus, also. Some interpretations encourage us to see Tess as specially marked out from all others. A less character-oriented reading emphasises a class of people, or even humanity in general.

Typical of the kind of confusion sometimes found in Hardy's thinking is his ambiguous presentation of the concept of 'Nature'. It will be remembered (see 'Survey': '"Social" approaches') that as long ago as 1894 Lionel Johnson remarked on this problem: 'What is this "Nature", of which or of whom, Mr Hardy speaks? . . . Is it a conscious Power? or a convenient name for the whole mass of physical facts?' (p.232). Johnson points out that it is somewhat naïve of Hardy to equate 'Nature' with anti-social life: 'Life "according to nature" means many things: Aristotle at least saw in the phrase nothing inconsistent with another phrase, that "man is by nature a social animal": just as Burke declared him to be "a religious animal"' (p.240).

A more detached treatment of the business is to be found in David Lodge's chapter on the language of *Tess* in his book *Language of Fiction* (see 'Survey': '"Formal" approaches'). He points out, following Ian Gregor, that there is a contradiction in *Tess*

between a 'Rousseauistic view of Nature' as essentially life-giving, healthy, opposed to the inhibiting, destructive forces of society and convention which alone generate human misery, and the 'deterministic view which Hardy runs alongside it', in which the world appears as a 'blighted star' and the three dairymaids in love with Angel 'writhed feverishly under the oppressiveness of an emotion which they neither expected nor desired'.   (p.172)

Hardy can scarcely hold both these viewpoints at once, and the contradiction spreads into the whole presentation of Tess herself. Hardy constantly associates her with images of 'natural' non-human things – birds, plants and animals – which lead us to believe she is specially a favourite of Nature. But in practical fact, as Lodge remarks, 'Nature is quite indifferent to Tess and her fate' (p.173). Again, the confusion seems to be in the very word 'Nature' itself. 'Nature' is rabbits hopping about and birds roosting, but it is also hills that Tess must climb, the ironically phallic-shaped stones at Flintcomb-Ash; it is decay and destruction, and, what is more 'natural' than anything else, it is death. So, while Hardy clearly wished us to see Tess as associated with a 'good' view of Nature, his own confusion about the term, particularly its relationship to Tess, leads us to feel unhappy about just what point he is trying to make.

The affective is based in the visual imagination

The affective approach tends to be contemplative rather than investigative. We investigate causes, trying to trace back a sequence of actions to their root. But the effect the novel has on us, how it moves its readers, is the outcome of their more passive appreciation of the scenes of the novel as they unfold. This is not to say that we remain unmoved by causal interpretations. We may be saddened or outraged by the revelation of society's indifference or hostility to Tess, but I would suggest that the true tragic experience, in this novel at least, lies in our appreciation of the effect such hostility has on the girl as we witness it from scene to scene of her pilgrimage. One might well substitute 'picture' for 'scene', indeed, since one of the strongest arguments for reading the novel affectively is the primacy of the visual imagination for Hardy. One can scarcely avoid an awareness of this from the very first page, where John Durbeyfield's appearance is caught for us with telling detail, down to the worn patch on his hat:

> He occasionally gave a smart nod, as if in confirmation of some opinion, though he was not thinking of anything in particular. An empty egg-basket was slung upon his arm, the nap of his hat was ruffled, a patch being quite worn away at its brim where his thumb came in taking it off.   [p.43]

And we are constantly made aware of colours, lights, shades, textures and shapes. But Hardy does more than simply evoke these qualities. He sees experience formed into pictures. On occasion, indeed, he refers to a specific picture by an artist, which demonstrates how his imagination worked at least as strongly through vision as through the mechanics of plotting, organising action. For example, when Tess and Marion are working at Flintcomb-Ash, he remarks after describing their figures that 'The pensive character which the curtained hood lent to their bent heads would have reminded the observer of some early Italian conception of the two Marys' [p.361].

The strikingness of such scenes is emphasised by their often being silent, so that there is no distraction from the visual quality. Such scenes do not merely punctuate the action: they give a definite shape to it, saying, 'here is the *state* of things now, without any speculation about why such things may have come about'. Such scenes act like a fuller version of Tony Tanner's linking of colours (see 'Survey': '"Formal" approaches'). They can anticipate and remind us of other scenes. For example, in chapter 22 all the hands at Talbothays Dairy are set to work quartering a meadow to root out the garlic which has tainted the milk: 'Differing one from another in natures and moods so greatly as they did, they yet formed, bending, a curiously uniform row – automatic, noiseless . . .' [p.196]. The scene reminds us of that at the beginning of chapter 14 when Tess helps with the reaping at Marlott while her baby is still alive. It also looks forward to the moment near the end of the novel when the law-officers who have quartered the country in their search for Tess appear one by one to surround her as she sleeps on the altar stone at Stonehenge. The 'weed' Tess has tainted a society which cannot tolerate her and which systematically destroys this 'foreign body' in its midst. The relationship between the three scenes is not causative, however, but relies on our placing the first two as 'omens', to use Tanner's word, for the last. There are also, of course, numerous omens throughout the book which are recognised by the characters themselves, notably by Tess. Their effect is again, I think, to focus our attention on effect rather than cause. Omens are signs of a mystical meaning in life. They cannot be justified by rational arguments of cause and effect, but are read directly and intuitively as pointers to some kind of destinty. In the novel it is not important whether they speak the truth or not. Their function is formal, suggesting how the future may be felt to be mysteriously contained in the present.

Hardy's poems' structure similar to his novels'

The emphasis an affective view places on pattern and symbol, the visual, the picture and the scene as the basis of the novel's structure may justify our calling it a 'poetic' interpretation. Hardy wrote poetry all his life, though he wrote no more novels after the publication of *Jude the Obscure* in 1895, and there is evidence that he saw himself primarily as a poet, novels being more important to him as a source of livelihood. Such a predilection on Hardy's part again points towards the validity of an affective interpretation. Many of Hardy's poems are based on just such scenes, moments and pictures as I have been discussing in *Tess,* and the similarity suggests that his imagination perhaps thought first in terms of striking moments, and only later was the plot constructed around them.

Importance of place in a scene

A particularly striking feature of Hardy's pictures is that they are almost inevitably of figures *in a landscape.* We see Tess dancing in a field, lying asleep in the Chase, wandering in the garden at Talbothays, labouring on the uplands at Flintcomb-Ash, lying on the sacrificial stone in the middle of Salisbury Plain. Place is at least as important as person. Sometimes, indeed, the landscape dwarfs the human figure. But the place on the geographical map of 'Wessex' is not so important as the place on what might be called the 'human map'. Each moment when we see the heroine against a new background represents some new stage in her 'pilgrimage'. Her emotional progress is marked by a scene which summarises what she is at that moment, gathers up all that has gone before, and often invites a contrast with her past self. Can we associate the sexless figure, bent before the driving rain, swede-hacking at Flintcomb-Ash, with the fresh, beautiful, seductive girl who danced at the club-walking in a field near Marlott? We *know* that the two are the same, but Hardy's contrasting pictures tell us the effects of time and experience. My point is that we do not know time as a thing measured by days and months so strongly as we know it measured in human suffering, and again the emphasis is thrown onto the series of moments, rather than the causes of those moments.

Tess's passivity favours an affective approach

I would suggest, finally, that Tess's own personality may be one of the most pressing reasons for reading the novel 'affectively'. While we cannot deny that she takes the initiative on a number of occasions and performs positive actions, many more of her most significant acts seem passive or negative. Even her decision to lie still in Angel's arms as he carries her across the swollen river in his sleep is a negative one. She will *not* commit suicide in case Clare falls with her. An act of strength and tenderness such as wringing the necks of the wounded birds is done in order to bring them sooner to death. On the larger scale, she seems a person to whom 'things happen'. The family's horse is run down while she is in charge of it; she passively is dressed up by her mother to visit her 'kin', and is seduced by Alec for her pains. She uncomplainingly allows herself to be cast off by her husband, and as a consequence is subjected to extreme physical hardship, which she stoically bears – almost, it would seem, as a propitiatory sacrifice to the absent Clare. Even her most positive act, the stabbing of d'Urberville, is the reaction of a despairing animal at bay, and of course is one which seals her doom. Rather than the tragic protagonist, it would surely be more accurate to term her the tragic victim, and, since our interest is focused so closely upon her, we are bound to appreciate the tragedy in terms of effects upon her, not the causes, which are many and varied. Her figure is at once the repository of suffering, moving through a landscape of bitter experience, and the focus for our own sense of tragedy, vouchsafed us in those moments with 'the figure in the landscape'.

'Stasis' illustrated in Tess's character

To summarise, then, while I would not claim that Hardy has written a novel with a Jamesian economy and strictness of form, *Tess* does seem to share some structural features with the work of the American novelist. Chief among these is that it works by pattern and symbol to form a 'poetic' structure which emphasises a certain staticness. I would disagree with Ian Gregor that we live through the book and find its form in the modification of our responses. My view would be closer to that of Tony Tanner, who emphasises the visual impact of *Tess*. I think we contemplate these images, rather than living through a story. Hardy's phrase 'a series of seemings' suggests for Gregor the idea of *process;* I would see the 'seemings' as pictures, and the implication to be of stasis rather than process. This does not mean, of course, that there is nothing dynamic or active in the novel, but I feel that Hardy tends to translate this dynamism into fixity – especially the moment, scene or picture.

As an example of what I mean by 'stasis', let me return for a moment to the character of Tess. Tess is in herself a celebration of many great human qualities. She is enduring, patient, has a purity of intention, humanity, courage and womanliness. But somehow we feel that these qualities are represented *through* her rather than acted out *by* her as part of individual human initiative. Irving Howe claims that, 'when the book is indeed fully alive, we have no wish to look beyond her or to think of her as representing anything whatever' (p.129). But I think that the very qualities for which Howe admires her – 'the potential of what life could be' (p.130) – are felt *as* pure qualities in which Tess's individuality is subordinated to her representation of general humanity. Howe himself recognises that the novel works as a series of scenes, with 'just enough plot loosely to thread together the several episodes that comprise the book': 'None of these panels is quite self-sufficient, since narrative tension accumulates from part to part; but each has a dinstinctiveness of place, action and tone which makes it profitable to think of the novel as episodic' (p.113),

Yet it seems to me that the idea of the 'panel' – the static picture – may well be carried into the matter of the heroine's character also. Returning, for example, to one of the most memorable scenes in which she appears, the swede-hacking at Flintcomb-Ash, we find a classic instance of the figure in the landscape. The two women are seen in the distance, the picture dominated by the earth and the sky:

Each leaf of the vegetable having already been consumed,

the whole field was in colour a desolate drab; it was a complexion without features, as if a face, from chin to brow, should be only an expanse of skin. The sky wore, in another colour, the same likeness; a white vacuity of countenance with the lineaments gone. So these two upper and nether visages confronted each other all day long, the white face looking down on the brown face, and the brown face looking up at the white face, without anything standing between them but the two girls crawling over the surface of the former like flies.   [p.360]

What strikes the reader most forcibly here, I think, is the distancing and anonymity of the scene. Neither sky nor earth is individualised, nor are the women. The effect of this is to bring out qualities of endurance and suffering, but not through the character of a particular girl actively engaged with life. Rather, Tess has become an object *representing* these qualities as part of a picture which would be incomplete without the setting of featureless earth and sky. 'Thus Tess walks on; a figure which is part of the landscape' [p.355]. Hardy's own words define his heroine and the way we are to apprehend her.

I shall now attempt the last two tasks of this study. The first of these is to suggest what kind of interpretation of *Tess* the 'affective' approach provides us with. The second is to decide what the relationship of such an approach is to the 'causative' side of the novel. Does it mean that we must ignore causes altogether, or may the two views be reconciled in some way? In fact the two problems are related, since, I think that to explain my affective interpretation will be to account for the place of causality to some extent. I shall therefore deal with matters as they arise, rather than strictly separating the two problems.

The inscrutability of causes in 'Tess'

If by 'causes' we mean an explanation for why things should be then Hardy's own comments are clear enough:

Why it was that upon this beautiful feminine tissue, sensitive as gossamer, and practically blank as snow as yet, there should have been traced such a coarse pattern as it was doomed to receive; why so often the coarse apropriates the finer thus, the wrong man the woman, the wrong woman the man, many thousand years of analytical philosophy have failed to explain to our sense of order.   [p.119]

And he goes on to reject the explanation of retribution as one to be 'scorned by average human nature'. Causes, in other words, are inscrutable in the last analysis, and this seems to me to be a point of view reinforced by the affective interpretation. The last paragraph of the novel summarises Hardy's ideas of the relationship between man and 'the way things are':

'Justice' was done, and the President of the Immortals, in Aeschylean phrase, had ended his sport with Tess. And the d'Urberville knights and dames slept on in their tombs unknowing. The two speechless gazers bent themselves down to the earth, as if in prayer, and remained thus a long time, absolutely motionless: the flag continued to wave silently. As soon as they had strength they arose, joined hands again, and went on.   [p.490]

I have already mentioned the 'President of the Immortals' and decided that he is only a substitute for the ineluctable ways of fate or chance. The sense of historical significance is also discounted. Tess Durbeyfield's ancestors are long dead, and know nothing of and care nothing for their descendant. The black flag which marks her terrible end waves silently and indifferently in the background. There is nothing for the two human beings in the scene to do but join hands (suggestive of human companionship) and go on (symbolic of human fortitude). The picture needs no words, and, indeed, words or explanations would reduce the 'message' from those largest truths at which Hardy is aiming. Even more explicit in its image of the inscrutable nature of things is the moment towards the end of the novel when Tess and Clare first come upon Stonehenge, as they feel their way through the darkness:

'What monstrous place is this?' said Angel.
'It hums', said she. 'Hearken!'
He listened. The wind, playing upon the edifice, produced a booming tune, like the note of some gigantic one-stringed harp. No other sound came from it, and lifting his hand and

advancing a step or two, Clare felt the vertical surface of the structure. It seemed to be of solid stone, without joint or moulding. Carrying his fingers onward he found that what he had come in contact with was a colossal rectangular pillar; by stretching out his left hand he could feel a similar one adjoining. At an indefinite height overhead something made the black sky blacker, which had the semblance of a vast architrave uniting the pillars horizontally. They carefully entered beneath and between; the surfaces echoed their soft rustle; but they seemed to be still out of doors. The place was roofless. Tess drew her breath fearfully, and Angel, perplexed, said –

'What can it be?' [pp.483–4]

The fact that it turns out to be part of Stonehenge naturally turns our minds towards worship, propitiation of the gods. But what gods were worshipped here, and were they susceptible of propitiation? The juxtaposition of the Victorian man and woman with the ancient monument identifies their problem, and the couple's incomprehension is a metaphor of their (and our) inability to make contact with the meaning of existence. The night is so dark that they are like blind people. They can hear a sound from the object, and can feel its surface and general shape. It towers above them, but does not give shelter, nor yield its extent or meaning. Again, no words are needed. Merely observing the picture of the two beneath the massive architrave, limited to their senses of touch and hearing by the darkness, is sufficient to convey the idea of an inscrutable presence.

Human insignificance

A further aspect of this scene is the way in which it contrasts the sizes of the human beings and the object. 'At an indefinite height overhead something made the black sky blacker' suggests an object whose dimensions are almost out of human measurement, at least in the darkness. Throughout *Tess* Hardy evokes the sense of human insignificance. It is not merely size which is involved, but depersonalisation. We have already seen Tess on the field at Flintcomb-Ash. Later, when she comes running after Clare, leaving the dead Alec d'Urberville behind her, Angel turns: 'The tape-like surface of the road diminished in his rear as far as he could see, and as he gazed a moving spot intruded on the white vacuity of its perspective' [p.473]. Again, Alec d'Urberville, coming to see Tess at Flintcomb-Ash, is first seen as a 'black speck':

> For hours nothing relieved the joyless monotony of things. Then, far beyond the ploughing-teams, a black speck was seen. It had come from the corner of a fence, where there was a gap, and its tendency was up the incline, towards the swede-cutters. From the proportions of a mere point it advanced to the shape of a ninepin . . . [p.392]

And when Angel wakes on Stonehenge he looks round to see 'something [that] seemed to move on the verge of the dip eastward – a mere dot. It was the head of a man approaching them from the hollow beyond the Sun-stone' [p.486].

The cumulative force of these images seems to me twofold. They distance us from the personal, composing human beings into a picture, and they suggest the insignificance, and even intrusiveness, of man in the world. A further interesting example of this depersonalising is to be found in the man who accompanies the threshing-machine, that 'tyrant that the women had come to serve' at Flintcomb-Ash:

> By the engine stood a dark motionless being, a sooty and grimy embodiment of tallness, in a sort of trance, with a heap of coals by his side: it was the engine-man. The isolation of his manner and colour lent him the appearance of a creature from Tophet, who had strayed into the pellucid smokelessness of this region of yellow grain and pale soil, with which he had nothing in common, to amaze and discompose its aborigines.   [pp.404–5]

This man is interesting because on one level he could be seen as an image of localised causality. He is part of that alien, tyrannical force of 'civilisation' which makes Tess its victim. She is natural to this landscape, the man is an intruder:

> He was in the agricultural world, but not of it . . .

> He spoke in a strange northern accent; his thoughts being

turned inwards upon himself, his eye on his iron charge,
hardly perceiving the scenes around him, and caring for
them not at all . . .   [p.405]

Undoubtedly he may be taken in this way, allowing for Hardy's
problems with concepts such as 'Nature', which I have already
discussed. But he seems to me also to be another image of that
alien intrusiveness by man upon the natural scene. He stands as
a mysterious figure, come we know not where from 'as if some
ancient doom compelled him to wander here against his will in
the service of his Plutonic master' [ibid.]. We may be reminded
of those other voyagers from unknown regions, the birds who
arrive in the frosty weather:

> gaunt spectral creatures with tragical eyes – eyes which had
> witnessed scenes of cataclysmal horror in inaccessible polar
> regions of a magnitude such as no human being had ever
> conceived, in curdling temperatures that no man could
> endure; which had beheld the crash of icebergs and the slide
> of snow-hills by the shooting light of the Aurora; been half
> blinded by the whirl of colossal storms and terraqueous
> distortions; and retained the expression of feature that such
> scenes had engendered. These nameless birds came quite
> near to Tess and Marian, but of all they had seen which
> humanity would never see, they brought no account. The
> traveller's ambition to tell was not theirs, and with dumb
> impassivity, they dismissed experiences which they did not
> value for the immediate incidents of this homely upland – the
> trivial movements of the two girls in disturbing the clods
> with their hackers so as to uncover something or other that
> these visitants relished as food.   [pp.363–4]

The engineer is at least a man, though a strange one, but these
birds seem to bring experiences from beyond humanity. Their
appearance speaks of a world of terrors transcending our
apprehension; and yet, like the silently waving flag over the
prison, or the massive architraves of Stonehenge, they tell
mankind nothing, looking no further than the food the women
can turn over for them. The peculiarly haunting quality of this
picture comes from the close association of a transcendent, vast
world of cataclysms and the 'trivial', earthly actions of the girls

as they hack at the swedes. This is important, and I use the word 'transcendent' deliberately, for, if we are invited to feel the insignificance of man in these images of alienation and depersonalisation, there is also running through *Tess* a strongly felt awareness of all that is *not* insignificant, and which points beyond the triviality of man in a particular time and place to our largest concerns – particularly what we may speculate about our final destiny.

The converse feeling of a transcendent reality

When Tess is working for Alec d'Urberville's mother, she finds one Saturday night that she must wait for a workpeople's dance to end before she may find company for her walk home. The couples spin round as she watches them, and, having now all found partners that suit them, they seem to become lost in their own movements for a few minutes: 'It was then that the ecstasy and the dream began, in which the emotion was the matter of the universe, and matter but an adventitious intrusion likely to hinder you from spinning where you wanted to spin' [p.108]. For a short while the dancers seem carried out of the earthly realm; matter becomes 'an adventitious intrusion'. Unfortunately, this state proves a temporary illusion:

> Suddenly there was a dull thump on the ground: a couple had fallen, and lay in a mixed heap. The next couple, unable to check its progress, came toppling over the obstacle. An inner cloud of dust rose around the prostrate figures amid the general one of the room, in which a twitching entanglement of arms and legs was discernible.   [Ibid.].

Such a farcical descent from the sublime must have been intended by Hardy, I feel, to suggest in a comic way how man *may* reach towards an escape from the unearthly, and may feel for a moment that he has attained it, but the pull of the earth is the pull of life, and while we are mortal will always overcome these transcendent moments. The scene is not a totally serious one, of course, but it is paralleled by other instances. One morning at Talbothays, Tess describes how she has had a kind of mystical or transcendent experience:

'I don't know about ghosts', she was saying; but I do know that our souls can be made to go outside our bodies when we alive.' . . .

'A very easy way to feel 'em go', continued Tess, 'is to lie on the grass at night and look straight up at some big bright star; and, by fixing your mind upon it, you will soon find that you are hundreds and hundreds o' miles away from your body, which you don't seem to want at all.'   [p.175]

Such a moment comes upon her 'without any determination of hers' when she hears Angel playing his harp:

Tess was conscious of neither time nor space. The exaltation which she had described as being producible at will by gazing at a star, came now without any determination of hers; she undulated upon the thin notes of the second-hand harp, and their harmonies passed like breezes through her, bringing tears into her eyes.   [p.179]

Such moments as this are opposed by Tess to the horror of 'real life', which seems to her to be a threatening series of expectations:

And you seem to see numbers of tomorrows just all in a line, the first of them the biggest and clearest, the others getting smaller and smaller as they stand father away; but they all seem very fierce and cruel and as if they said, 'I'm coming! Beware of me! Beware of me!' . . . But *you* sir, can raise up dreams with your music, and drive all such horrid fancies away!   [p.180]

There are further hints of such curious states throughout the novel – all, I think, pertaining to Tess, and all suggesting that there is a disjunction between soul and body, and that it is possible at times to be aware of that larger state of being comprehended in the first of these two things. The moments are 'affective' in two ways. First, they are known personally through the sensations of the individual character – they affect the subjective consciousness. Secondly, they affect us, the readers, as parts of the meaning of the work of art. They do not explain the nature of the sensation, but they emotionally convince us of the nature of being. We are not inclined to investigate, but are prepared to accept the moment as an image of a deeper truth than may be explained away by searching for causes. It seems to me that such enlarging of the questions and concerns of life is a crucial part of the meaning an affective interpretation gives to the novel. It also gives some suggestions as to how causality may be reconciled to such an approach. I shall now therefore attempt to define some of the meaning expressed in these images of great, general human concerns.

Tragedy inevitable in the human condition

Basically, *Tess of the d'Urbervilles*, read affectively, presents the causes of Tess's tragedy as being finally an inevitable part of the human condition, rather than a matter of localised concerns such as economic conditions or ideas of the late nineteenth century, or the exploitation of women by men, or the failings of a particular character. The 'human condition' as Hardy sees it is broadly one where man is somehow at odds with, or the victim of, his world. When I say 'world' I am not referring to the social world, nor even to the world of 'Nature', but to the whole of 'the way things are'. Among the most striking feelings to which man is subject in *Tess* is a sense of isolation and transcience in an indifferent world. Again, it is most frequently Tess herself whose sensibility conveys this feeling to us. When she goes to church after her 'fall', one of her favourite psalm-settings happens to be sung – 'the old double chant "Langdon"':

> but she did not know what it was called, though she would much have liked to know. She thought, without exactly wording the thought, how strange and godlike was a composer's power, who from the grave could lead through sequences of emotion, which he alone had felt at first, a girl like her who had never heard of his name, and never would have a clue to his personality.   [p.134]

We have here again something of that transcendent faculty I observed before in Tess, but added to it her feeling of isolation from the composer. She is moved, but moved alone; the composer will never be known to her in himself. A similar feeling is evoked when she thinks of the people in London who will enjoy the milk from Talbothays:

> Tess was so receptive that the few minutes of contact with the whirl of material progress lingered in her thought.
> 'Londoners will drink it at their breakfasts tomorrow, won't they?' she asked. 'Strange people that we have never seen.' . . .
> 'Who don't know anything of us, and where it comes from; or think how we two drove miles across the moor to-night in the rain that it might reach 'em in time?'   [pp.251–2]

Her personal transience is suggested many times. For example, when she goes to work at Talbothays we are told,

> Her kindred dwelling there would probably continue their daily lives as heretofore, with no great diminution of pleasure in their consciousness, although she would be far off, and they deprived of her smile. In a few days the children would engage in their games as merrily as ever without the sense of any gap left by her depature.   [p.155]

This temporary parting is more gloomily extended on some occasions to the greatest parting, from which there is no return:

> She suddenly thought one afternoon, when looking in the glass at her fairness, that there was yet another date, of greater important to her than those; that of her own death, when all these charms would have disappeared; a day which lay sly and unseen among all the other days of the year, giving no sign or sound when she annually passed over it; but not the less surely there.   [pp.149–50]

People living on, who knew the date of her demise, would, she reflects, find 'nothing singular' in remarking upon it.

Four large 'causes' inherent in being human

Death is one of the fundamental truths illuminated in this novel. It is suggested in Tess laid in the stone coffin by Clare and her lying on the altar at Stonehenge, as well as in many of her own moments of perception. It illustrates neatly the difference between causality and the affective. We have seen that Tess may have a self-destructive urge. She asks why she is "on the wrong side of this door" at the d'Urberville tomb, says that she likes to be at Stonehenge, and when the law overtakes her, says, "It is as it should be, . . . Angel, I am almost glad – yes glad! This happiness could not have lasted. It was too much. I have had enough; and now I shall not live for you to despise me!" [p.487].

This inclination towards death is a personal thing; a part of Tess's nature. On the other hand, the general fact of death for all people is what is embodied in the affective reading. Both, in a sense, express a cause, but Tess's character is a particular and localised factor. Death as a phenomenon we all experience in common is so large a cause as to be finally inscrutable. Death and dissolution await us all, and no more and no less can be said. But against death is set the fundamental drive in human beings which makes them go on. The memory of Talbothays, and in Tess's case the hope of renewing the life she lived there, animate both her and Marian when they are working at Flintcomb-Ash:

> 'You can see a gleam of a hill within a few miles o' Froom Valley from here when 'tis fine', said Marian.
> 'Ah! Can you?' said Tess, awake to the new value of this locality.   [p.362]

And Hardy comments 'So the two forces were at work here as everywhere, the inherent will to enjoy, and the circumstantial will against enjoyment' [ibid].

He explicitly assigns the two forces to 'everywhere'. They are fundamental to all human experience, and we feel their rhythms running through the book. Rhythm is one of the most difficult concepts to speak of in the novel, but it is fundamental to an affective interpretation. Through Tess's consciousness (as so often) we feel the alternating pulse of natural human vitality and hope and the intransigence of circumstances – 'the way things are'. We feel it in Tess's first naïve freshness and unconscious provocativeness, which is so soon followed by her grief at loss of both virginity and the baby. But hope returns in

'The Rally', rising to the climax of the revelation of her past to Clare. Her spirits swing back through resignation and fortitude to despair, only to be freed finally for a few days of calm in which her own spirit seems to find the peace it has been seeking throughout. It will be appreciated that here again we are not being invited to look for causes, but are invited only to feel the rhythm of life in the 'pilgrimage' of one person.

Purgation of tragic emotions

The impermanence and isolation of the self, the inevitability of death, the intransigence of circumstances and the unquench-able will of human beings to survive and seek joy – these are the large truths about 'the state of things' that Hardy's vision presents us with. But there is another aspect of the affective approach to tragedy: namely, that comprehended in Aristotle's theory of the purgation of emotions. 'Pity and fear' are the Greek philosopher's tragic emotions, and we undoubtedly feel something of both these in Tess, particularly the former. Perhaps more powerful than either of these emotions, however, is that feeling comprehended by the word 'sadness', stretching from the intensity of grief at one pole to the relative softness of regret at the other. We may feel sadness as a direct result of reading episodes in the book, but I think by far the most poignant moments are again embodied in scenes and incidents, where the action composes itself into a little picture, to be contemplated rather than entered into. The detachment achieved thereby is also a crucial means of drawing our attention to a further great truth. This, perhaps the most important of all in *Tess,* is the inescapable truth of time.

I have already drawn attention to the first encounter between Clare and Tess at the club-dancing, when he neglected to choose her as his partner. As he hurries away to rejoin his brothers, he momentarily looks back:

> On account of his long delay he started in a flying-run down the lane westward, and had soon passed the hollow and mounted the next rise. He had not yet overtaken his brothers, but he paused to get breath, and looked back. He could see the white figures of the girls in the green enclosure whirling about as they had whirled when he was among

them. They seemed to have quite forgotten him already. [p.54]

Seeing Tess standing 'apart by the hedge alone' he regrets not having asked her to dance, but bows to the inevitable – 'it could not be helped' – and continues his journey and his life. The moment of passing from one phase of life to another is captured many times in *Tess*. When she first leaves her parents' home, we are told that 'the Vale of Blackmoor was to her the world, and its inhabitants the races thereof' [p.75]. But now she is looking out of the valley:

> Every contour of the surrounding hills was as personal to her as that of her relatives' faces; but for what lay beyond her judgement was dependent on the teaching of the village school, where she had held a leading place at the time of her leaving, a year or two before this date.   [Ibid.].

At the beginning of the 'Maiden No More' section she pauses on the height between the two worlds of her innocence and her deception, looking down into Blackmoor Vale with new eyes. With 'The Rally' we see her departing from her home a second time, and looking back 'regretfully at Marlott and her father's house, although she had been so anxious to get away' [p.155]. Space might be said to represent time here, her journeys on foot being her journeys in experience. But there is also an emotional association attached to these moments in which the past is juxtaposed with the present. Like Clare she feels regret as she looks back, and the act of looking back is caught again for Clare when he turns to see her running after him down the road when she has murdered Alec, and finally when he turns with Liza-Lu to see Tess's ultimate fate in an all-embracing panorama:

> When they had nearly reached the top of the great West Hill the clocks in the town struck eight. Each gave a start at the notes, and, walking onwards yet a few steps, they reached the first milestone, standing whitely on the green margin of the grass, and backed by the down, which here was open to the road. They entered upon the turf, and, impelled by a force that seemed to overrule their will, suddenly stood still, turned, and waited in paralyzed suspense beside the stone. [pp.488–9]

Choice in 'Tess' is affective rather than causative

The figure half-turned to look back becomes an image of regret for opportunities missed and potential unfulfilled. More than this, it symbolises that essential ingredient of tragedy, the sense of inevitability. The act, whether it be not dancing, having an illegitimate child, or murdering Alec, has been done, and is now our 'Fate' catching up with us, as Tess catches up with Angel. She brings fulfilment, but it is a tragic fulfilment, whose threads are only finally drawn together with her execution. The emotion – regret – therefore has superadded to it the terrible poignancy of inevitability. Such poignancy seems to me quite to transcend Roy Morrell's assertion that it is the moral failure in making choices which represents the main tragedy of the novel. Certainly the lack of a firm purpose on Tess's part at certain moments may be a localised cause, but it is subsumed in the cumulative images of regret at something we have witnessed without being able to change it. And we cannot change it because such happenings are in the nature of things. What I am suggesting is that choice is certainly present as a factor in *Tess,* but not as a matter of moral censure. Rather it is something which throws our attention onto the *effect* – the terrible and inevitable wrongness (not moral wrongness) of the choice. The emphasis which Hardy lays on the moment of choice is not to draw our attention to Tess's moral failing, but to make her ultimate error of judgement (for example, mistiming the telling of her story to Clare) the more painful. In a passage such as the following, we surely feel nothing but pity for Tess, and an understanding of why she so desperately wanted to tell Angel but tragically could not until it was too late:

> They [the other milkmaids] were not aware that, at these words, salt, stinging tears trickled down upon Tess's pillow anew, and how she resolved, with a bursting heart, to tell all her history to Angel Clare, despite her mother's command – to let him for whom she lived and breathed despise her if he would, and her mother regard her as a fool, rather than preserve a silence which might be deemed a treachery to him, and which somehow seemed a wrong to these. [p.265]

I have referred several times to 'the way things are' or 'the nature of things', suggesting that it is to this larger order of causality that an affective view of the novel refers us. But is there any way in which we feel this larger order as something more than simply an abstraction meaning more or less 'that's life'? There is, I think, and I shall end my discussion of the merits of causal and affective approaches with an examination of the way in which Hardy captures the 'nature of things', because it seems to me not only the most effective reconciliation of the two approaches, but also one of the most profound aspects of Hardy's art.

The intransigence of life

When he is philosophising about 'Nature' as a force, or about some abstract entity, Hardy, as we have seen, can be confused and confusing. But in particular instances of the intransigence of things and conditions we can be in no doubt of their 'meaning'. They 'mean', in fact, nothing beyond themselves. Returning yet again to the scenes on the uplands of Flintcomb-Ash, we see Tess exposed to all the rigours of that 'starveacre' place. While they are swede-hacking the rain comes on:

> and Marian said that they need not work any more. But if they did not work they would not be paid; so they worked on. It was so high a situation, this field, that the rain had no occasion to fall, but raced along horizontally upon the yelling wind, sticking into them like glass splinters till they were wet through. Tess had not known till now what was really meant by that. There are degrees of dampness, and a very little is called being wet through in common talk. But to stand working slowly in a field, and feel the creep of rain-water, first in leg and shoulders, then on hips and head, then at back, front, and sides, and yet to work on till the leaden light diminishes and marks that the sun is down, demands a distinct modicum of stoicism, even of valour.   [p.361]

The cruel necessity of their work is suggested by 'if they did not work they would not be paid', but it is the actual physical quality of the soaking, penetrating rain which carries the most powerful suggestion of necessity here. The rain does not, however, 'stand for' anything beyond the 'nature of things'. As Shakespeare said, 'the rain it raineth every day', and what we understand is that the pain of living is as natural as weather. After rain there is intense frost, in which 'even their thick leather gloves could not prevent the frozen masses they handled from biting their fingers' [p.362]. Later again:

> one day a peculiar quality invaded the air of this open country. There came a moisture which was not of rain, and a cold which was not of frost. It chilled the eyeballs of the twain, made their brows ache, penetrated to their skeletons, affecting the surface of the body less than its core. They knew that it meant snow, and in the night the snow came. [p.364]

The girls do not know why or from where the snow comes, but they know it *will* come, and this again emphasises inescapable necessity. Snow is a part of winter just as naturally as sunshine and warmth are part of summer.

The earth stands most powerfully for this intransigence

Dorothy Van Ghent, in a sensitive and powerful study of *Tess* (1953), has posited the earth itself as 'the most primitive antagonist of consciousness' (p.201). She points to its 'clogging action', 'defying conscious motive', or at Talbothays 'conspiring with its ancient sensuality to provoke instinct', or at Flintcomb-Ash 'demoralizing consciousness by its mere geological flintiness' (p.201). This seems to me to be a part of that apprehension of the 'nature of things' which also includes the sun, the rain and the snow. Van Ghent points out also that the earth as a thing to be traversed is 'a factor of causation: 'and by this we refer simply to the long stretches of earth that have to be trudged in order that a person may get from one place to another, the slowness of the business, the irreducible reality of it (for one has only one's feet)' (ibid.). The point is, though, that as a cause the distances to be traversed do not here stand for anything but themselves:

> In *Tess* the earth is *primarily not a metaphor but a real thing* that one has to move on in order to get anywhere or do anything, and it constantly acts in its own motivating, causational substantiality by being there in the way of human purposes

to encounter, to harass them, detour them, seduce them, defeat them.   (p.202)

Journeying, here, is not even that symbolic pilgrimage of experience we mentioned earlier. It is simply and finally and irreducibly itself, and in this it is the profoundest cause and the profoundest effect. It is profoundly affective because it makes us feel, directly as upon our own bodies, physical sensations – especially of pain. We feel with Tess and Marian the rain, frost and snow. We feel also the weariness and exhaustion involved in walking long distances when one is footsore, one's burden is heavy and one has had to rise at 2 o'clock in the morning. The physically tangible moments of the novel are perhaps the most memorable feature of *Tess*. Hardy feels intensely with his heroine at moments such as this when she reaches Flintcomb-Ash:

> The wall felt warm to her back and shoulders, and she found that immediately within the gable was the cottage fireplace, the heat of which came through the bricks. She warmed her hands upon them, and also put her cheek – red and moist with the drizzle – against their comforting surface.   [p.356]

The threshing-machine may symbolise many things, but finally it is the physical suffering of Tess, meaning nothing *except* the human body's capacity to be fatigued, which sticks in our memories:

> Tess left her post, her knees trembling so wretchedly with the shaking of the machine that she could scarcely walk.   [p.407]

> She could not get her morsels of food down her throat; her lips were dry, and she was ready to choke.   [p.410]

> A panting ache ran through the rick. The man who fed was weary, and Tess could see that the red nape of his neck was encrusted with dirt and husks.   [p.413]

But, seen as a cause, this suffering is equally profound, being what Dorothy Van Ghent calls 'the causes of causes'. When we have stripped away second causes such as society's laws, character, the ideas and conditions of the age, history, we must feel that these are only incidental manifestations of that final cause which is so deeply woven into the fabric of being that it can scarcely be called a cause. Certainly we cannot identify it by name, as we can the secondary causes, and thereby 'explain' the tragedy. It is this which makes *Tess* profoundly tragic: we are made to know that for man to be man he must suffer, and no explanation, blame or palliation can change that fact.

Summary: individual and general tragedy

Throughout the 'Appraisal' I have emphasised the contrast between 'causal' and 'affective' approaches to *Tess of the d'Urbervilles*. Such a clear-cut division was necessary for the conduct of my argument, but in fact the divide is not so absolute as might appear. I hope that I have shown how an affective approach may assimilate local causes to some extent and make them attributes of the real heart of the novel, which is its power to evoke large and timeless feelings about human suffering, death, and the nature of things. Yet I would not have the reader leave this study with the feeling that the particularity of causal interpretations has been swept aside in the pursuit of more static, contemplative, 'poetic' approaches. To say that the profoundest aspect of this novel transcends particular time and place is not to take it *out of* time and place. This is a tragedy of late-Victorian England. It is not interchangeable with *Oedipus Rex* or *Hamlet*, although the pity and fear evoked in the audience may be much the same in all cases. It is a special feature of the novel as a form that it derives its meaning from its contemporaneity. Its vital message is expressed through the ideas, the manners, even so localised a feature as the means of transport, of its age. All that I have said about the travelling figure in a landscape would be nullified if the novel were to be set in an age where walking was not a necessity for a country girl. Tess would not be hanged in 1985. She might not have been seduced. If she had been, her guilt would not be so overwhelming as it is for the Victorian maiden. The circumstantial detail of reality is not merely a background against which a timeless tragedy is played out. It is an integral part of the whole meaning – the expression of a particular time and place and person. As a demonstration of this point we cannot do better than return finally to the heroine herself, for without a sense of her reality, as I suggested in the Introduction, the book is nothing. She is purity, fortitude, womanliness and suffering embodied, and yet beyond this she is herself and no other person. Her voice, her mouth, her gestures are part of a uniqueness which is of the essence of tragedy. Tess may have had that practised on her which her ancestors had carried out on other girls centuries before, but 'that does not mend the matter', because we are concerned with her single fate. She shares the common lot of all mankind – to suffer and endure and love. But it is Hardy's genius to make us feel that her pain is no less unique for all that – as unique as Tess was for him. That the sense of her being was so strong for Hardy as to seep into his 'real' life should not surprise us when we understand that in her special vitality we apprehend the universality and the uniqueness of tragedy.

References

The following are listed under the sections of the book to which they appertain, followed by a page reference for the first quotation from them in the text. In some cases works for further reference have been added to a section.

'Social' Approaches
Kettle, Arnold, *An Introduction to the English Novel* (2 vols. London, 1951, reprinted 1965). Vol. II, chapter IV, 'Hardy: *Tess of the D'Urbervilles'* p.51.
Williams, Raymond, *The English Novel, from Dickens to Lawrence* (London, 1970), p.102.
Johnson, Lionel, *The Art of Thomas Hardy* (London, 1894; new edition, London, 1923), p.233.
see also:
Enstice, Andrew, *Thomas Hardy: Landscapes of the Mind* (London, 1979).

'Character' Approaches
Morrell, Roy, *Thomas Hardy, the Will and the Way* (Kuala Lumpur, 1965) p.18.
Howe, Irving, *Thomas Hardy* (New York, 1966; Collier Books edition, New York, 1973), p.131.
Sankey, Benjamin, *The Major Novels of Thomas Hardy* (Denver 1965). pp.33-36 reprinted in *Twentieth Century Interpretations of 'Tess of the D'Urbervilles'* edited by Albert J. La Valley (Englewood Cliffs, 1969), p.98.
Lawrence, D.H. 'Study of Thomas Hardy', in *Phoenix, the Posthumous Papers of D.H. Lawrence*, edited by Edward D. McDonald (London, 1936, reprinted 1967), p.487.
see also:
Thurley, Geoffrey, *The Psychology of Hardy's novels* (University of Queensland Press, 1975).
Hyman, Virginia R. *Ethical Perspective in the Novels of Thomas Hardy* (New York and London, 1975).

'Ideas' Approaches
De Laura, David J. '"The Ache of Modernism" in Hardy's Later Novels', *ELH* Vol. 34, No. 3 (Sept. 1967), pp.380-399. p.380.
see also:
Holloway, John, *The Victorian Sage* (London, 1953).
Rutland, William, *Thomas Hardy, A Study of his Writings and Background* (Oxford, 1938).
Webster, Harvey C. *On a Darkling Plain* (Chicago, 1947).

'Formal' Approaches
James, Henry, Letter to Hugh Walpole, May 19th, 1912. *The Letters of Henry James*, selected and edited by Percy Lubbock (London, 1920), Vol. II, p.246.
Gregor, Ian, *The Great Web* (London, 1974), p.32.

Tanner, Tony, 'Colour and Movement in Hardy's *Tess of the D'Urbervilles*', CQ Vol.10, No.3 (1968), pp. 219-239. p.219.
Lodge, David, *Language of Fiction* (London, 1966), p.47.
see also:
Kramer, Dale, *Thomas Hardy: the Forms of Tragedy* (Michigan and London, 1975).
Miller, J. Hillis, *Thomas Hardy, Distance and Desire* (Cambridge), Mass. 1970).

A Genetic Approach
Laird, J.T. *The Shaping of 'Tess of the D'Urbervilles'* (Oxford, 1975).
see also:
Purdy, Richard L. *Thomas Hardy: A Bibliographical Study* (Oxford, 1954. Reprinted, 1979).
Chase, Mary Ellen, *Thomas Hardy from Serial to Novel* (1927, reissued New York, 1964).

'Appraisal'
Aristotle, *On the Art of Poetry,* in *Classical Literary Criticism,* translated by T.S. Dorsch, Penguin Classics (Harmondsworth, 1965), p.39.
Van Ghent, Dorothy, *The English Novel, Form and Function* (New York, 1953), p.201.

Selected Bibliography

Much of the secondary material referred to in this book is to be found, in whole or in part, in:
R.P. Draper (ed.) *Hardy: the Tragic Novels* ('Casebook' series London, 1975, repr. 1983),
and in:
Albert J. La Valley (ed.) *Twentieth Century Interpretations of 'Tess of the D'Urbervilles'* (Englewood Cliffs, N.J. 1969).

Many of the books listed under 'References' would repay reading in full, especially perhaps Irving Howe's study, which is one of the best introductions to the whole Hardy *oeuvre*.
Hardy, Thomas, *The Life and Work of Thomas Hardy*, ed. Michael Milgate (London, 1984).
    This autobiography, originally published under Hardy's wife's name, could be read in company with a modern life such as that by Robert Gittings: *Young Thomas Hardy* (London, 1975) and *The Older Hardy* (London, 1978).
see also:
R.G. Cox (ed.) *Thomas Hardy, the Critical Heritage* (London, 1970).

Michael Milgate, *Thomas Hardy, His Career as a Novelist* (London, 1971).
John Bayley, 'An Essay on Hardy' (Cambridge, 1978)
J.I.M. Stewart, *Thomas Hardy* (London, 1971).
John Holloway, *The Charted Mirror* (London, 1960). Contains two interesting essays on Hardy.
A.J. Guerard, *Hardy: the Novels and Stories* (Cambridge, 1949).
Douglas Brown, *Thomas Hardy* (London, 1954, reprinted 1961).
    These last two are earlier studies which have dated a little, but are still worth consulting for their general common-sense.

84

Index

Aristotle, 53, 57, 73
De Laura, David J., 23ff, 50, 53
Gregor, Ian, 23, 34ff, 42, 62
Howe, Irving, 14, 15, 52, 53, 62
James, Henry, 31ff, 36, 52, 61
Johnson, Lionel, 10, 22, 57
Kettle, Arnold, 1ff, 51, 52, 53
Laird, J.T., 43ff

Lawrence, D.H., 6, 17ff, 50, 52
Lodge, David, 40ff, 52, 57, 58
Morrell, Roy, 11ff, 52, 53, 75
Sankey, Benjamin, 16
Tanner, Tony, 36ff, 59
Van Ghent, Dorothy, 77, 78
Williams, Raymond, 4ff, 51, 52